S0-BEZ-272

LOVE'S HARVEST
The Life of Blessed Pauline

By
Frederick A. Farace, S.T.L.

Edited by
Joe Kindel and Bonnie Lewis

Published by
THE RIEHLE FOUNDATION
P.O. Box 7
Milford, Ohio 45150

Published by The Riehle Foundation.

For additional copies of this book, individuals may contact:
    The Riehle Foundation
    P.O. Box 7
    Milford, Ohio 45150

Bookstores and distributors should contact:
    Faith Publishing Company
    P.O. Box 237
    Milford, Ohio 45150

Copyright © 1994: Frederick A. Farace, S.T.L.

Cover photo by M. Kindel.

Library of Congress Catalog Card No.: 94-061408

ISBN: 1-877678-31-7

Dedicated to Albert Visintainer
who first told me about his cousin
Mother Pauline Visintainer

Mother Pauline at the age of 24.

Contents

Preface

The "communion of saints" is a phrase we have grown up with. What does it really mean to the 21st century Christian? Who are the saints? Why have saints? In this cynical age, the world needs heroes, but where are they to be found? The celebrities of sports, politics, government, war or entertainment usually send us the wrong signals. What we need are hope, trust, confidence, optimism and the virtue of true love. This is why the Church introduced the beatification and canonization of Christians who have manifested heroic virtue. Not only are the saints models to be imitated, but they have shown, after their death, the power of intercession with the heavenly Father. Two good signs of this intercessory power are the growth of a following in the saints' honor, and miracles performed in their name.

This book is about one of these heroes—Amabile Visintainer, who became a saint. In order to know more about Amabile, I lived in her adopted land of Brazil for a few months. I was able to see how Amabile Visintainer, an illiterate, untutored child, was able to become a modern day foundress of a great congregation. She became the loving, humble and holy Mother Pauline of the Agonizing Heart of Jesus.

Our Holy Father, Pope John Paul II, recognizing the virtues of Mother Pauline, and the love and esteem shown to her by the Brazilian people, solemnly beatified her on October 18, 1991 before hundreds of thousands of people in the city of Florianopolis, in the state of Santa Catarina, in the largest Catholic country of the world, Brazil.

There are two biographies of Mother Pauline written in Portuguese and translated into Spanish and Italian: *Madre Paulina, A Coloninha,* by Fidelis Dalcin Barbosa and *Essere-Per-Gli-Altri,* by Sister Celia B. Cadorin of the Little Sisters of the Immaculate Conception. I have referred to these biographies for some information and I have also used the archives and the published history of the Congregation of the Little Sisters of the Immaculate Conception, *Historia Da Congregacao,* by Mother Mary Doroteia of the Little Sisters of the Immaculate Conception.

I have visited the foundations of the Little Sisters throughout Brazil, particularly those founded by Mother Pauline during the period when she was Superior General.

A tremendous source of information for me was speaking to the many Sisters who knew and lived with Mother Pauline who are now retired from active ministry.

While many religious orders have suffered a decline in numbers since the turbulent times of the sixties, the Little Sisters have increased in number from 1,153 in 1965 to 1,892 today. This is a good indication that the original fire of love of Mother Pauline is continuing to burn in the hearts of her Sisters. On December 7, 1995, the Little Sisters of the Immaculate Conception will celebrate the 100th anniversary of the investiture and personal consecration of the original three girls; one hundred years of bringing in love's harvest.

—Frederick A. Farace, S.T.L.

*Statue of the 18 year old Amabile Visintainer
in Nova Trento.*

*The house where Mother Pauline was born
in Vigolo Vattaro, Italy.*

The first convent and infirmary at Vigolo, Brazil.

The second convent in Nova Trento, Brazil.

The first three Sisters of the Congregation. From left to right: Sister Agnes (Teresa Maoli), Mother Pauline, and Mother Matilda (Virginia Nicolodi).

Fr. Louis Rossi, co-founder of the Little Sisters of the Immaculate Conception.

*Mother Pauline shortly before the
amputation of her arm.*

The statue of Mother Pauline atop the mountain overlooking the valley where she began her work. She carries a hoe and a cross.

The shrine of Mother Pauline at Vigolo near Nova Trento, Brazil.

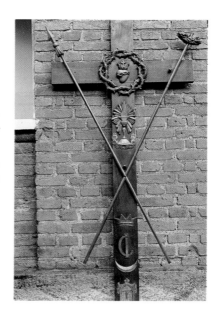

The Community Cross of the Little Sisters of the Immaculate Conception fashioned by Mother Pauline and Fr. Rossi.

The inner courtyard of the motherhouse in São Paulo, Brazil.

Mother Pauline (center) with her novices in 1941 at the motherhouse in São Paulo, Brazil.

CHAPTER 1

The Early Life of Amabile Visintainer

Amabile (pronounced ahm-AH-bee-lay) Lucia Visintainer was born on December 16, 1865, in Vigolo Vattaro, Trento, in present-day northern Italy. She was the second child and first daughter of 14 children, of whom 8 survived.

Her father, Antonio Napoleone Visintainer, was known and called only by the name Napoleone. He was a skilled stonemason and bricklayer. He was known by all as a kind, hardworking, and compassionate man of profound faith. His wife, Anna Pianezzar, was generous and deeply pious, a good wife and mother.

Amabile grew up in Vigolo Vattaro surrounded by friends and relatives. Practically everyone was in some way related either by marriage or blood relation. There was a close bond of friendship in the small town. Because of the custom of choosing godparents for the sacraments of Baptism and Confirmation, families were also spiritually bonded.

Very little is known about Amabile's early childhood until about eight years of age when she received the sacrament of Confirmation with her older brother, Ernesto, and her younger sister, Domenica. In those days, the practice of the Church was to confer the sacrament of Confirmation before the sacraments of Penance and Holy Eucharist.

Amabile was a gentle, sweet girl loved by everyone. At eight years of age, she went to work in the silk mill, which was located in Vigolo Vattaro. Since the family was poor, it was necessary for Amabile to begin work at an early age. Some families were so destitute that the children were the only wage-earners in the family. The lack of work in Vigolo Vattaro forced Amabile's father, Napoleone, to leave home for many months at a time in order to seek work throughout the Tyrol. His family sorely missed him. They needed him to be with them. Something had to be done. It was at this time that Napoleone began to hear friends speaking of immigration to America.

In 1824 there was a flood of emigration from Germany to Brazil, followed by the Austrians who spoke German. In 1875 a wave of emigration began from northern Italy and the Tyrol. The government of Brazil, after the Act of Independence from Portugal, invited Europeans to settle in Brazil. The Brazilian Government offered fertile land and the opportunity to own as much land as one was able to work. Many stories abounded of a land "flowing with milk and honey." A frequent topic of conversation in the Tyrol and in northern Italy was "are you going to Brazil?" "Are you going to Argentina?"

Amabile, who was only eight years old at the time, retained vivid memories of her early childhood in Vigolo Vattaro, Italy. Her letters are full of information about those days of crisis for her family and neighbors. They speak of the poverty, the hunger, the exploitation of children, the sadness of parents and the uprooting of families from a place they had lived for generations.

When Amabile was eight years old and had started to work in the silk mill, her mother would give her a lunch of cheese and bread to eat at the mill. Anna was very proud of her energetic little girl who insisted that she work to help the family. She used to call Amabile "Amabilotta" which, freely translated from the Italian, means "Mommy's big girl." After a few weeks of work, Anna noticed that her Amabile was getting pale and thin. Thinking she was working too hard, Anna asked Amabile how she felt and why she looked so drawn. Amabile said she felt fine and that work was not hard. Her mother persisted, wanting to know why Amabile was losing weight and becoming pale. Finally, Amabile admitted that she had been giving away her lunch to others. She said, "Mommy, there are such poor girls in the factory who have nothing to eat. They never bring anything to eat because their families have no food." Amabile not only shared but gave her entire lunch to those who needed it. She said they needed it more than she did. The poorest of the poor helping the poor! This was going to be the story of Amabile's life. A poor little country girl loving God and seeing Christ in others, loving everyone because all are the children of God. When Amabile's mother chided her for giving her lunch away she said, "Mommy, didn't Jesus tell us to give unto others? It gives me such joy to see the other girls eat and enjoy what I give them!"

Anna was an untiring worker. She was strong and patient in taking care of the needs of the family while her husband was working far from home. All the daily responsibility of raising the family was upon her plus the care of Napoleone's dear mother who was very ill. When Amabile saw that her mother was pregnant and weak, she decided to take some of the burden from her mother by caring for dear Nonna (Grandmother). Anna was very reluctant, but Amabile began by rising early before going to the factory and washing her grandmother and feeding her. Each day after work, Amabile would hurry home to clean Grandmother's room, wash her clothing and bed linens and give her supper. Amabile would sing to her, and they prayed together. Her grandmother called Amabile "my little Angel." She said it was like being in Heaven to be near her loving granddaughter.

After Anna saw how thin and pale Amabile was becoming, she decided that Amabile must give up some of her work. It was too much for a child of her age. Caring for Nonna and working at the factory were sapping her strength. Anna wanted to get someone else to care for Nonna. Amabile pleaded with her mother not to take this away from her; she loved Nonna and felt great joy taking care of her. The grandmother also begged Anna not to take her little angel from her. Nonna said Amabile was her salvation, and she did not have much more time to live. Nonna constantly prayed that she would die before they immigrated to America. Anna relented and Amabile happily cared for her grandmother until Nonna died.

Napoleone and Anna, after much prayer and agonizing, had come to a decision. In order to give their children a better life and increase their opportunity to live without the specter of famine and fear, they would go to Brazil with their many neighbors and countrymen. The first task was to save enough money for passage. The government of Brazil had promised to give them land, but they had to save money for supplies and other needs before establishing a homestead. Napoleone had to leave home for six more months to find work as a stonemason and bricklayer in other parts of the Tyrol. When he returned, there would certainly be enough for their passage.

Amabile was very excited. She had heard so many stories of the new world—how wonderful it would be! There would be enough food, warmth, and money to live. Best of all, Daddy would be with them all the time. He would not have to leave home for long periods of time again. She was not worried or concerned. God would help them. He would show them the way. Amabile always had a special wisdom and trust, no matter how difficult the odds seemed to be. How amazing that this little country girl was able to say so frequently the words, "We must love Jesus and nothing more." These words were to become the driving force of her life. Later on, as Mother Pauline, she would begin every letter with these very words.

The emigration from Vigolo Vattaro for the first group of 130 persons began August 1, 1875. Napoleone and Anna, with their children and Anna's mother, father and brothers, were to leave on September 25, 1875. Those who remained were saddened by the vast immigration of the Trentini to the New World. Before the families departed for America, the archbishop went to the parish churches of each town in the Archdiocese of Trent to celebrate Mass and confirm the children. During the sacrament of Confirmation at St. George's Parish in Vigolo Vattaro, the archbishop gave a very moving sermon to the families about to leave their homeland. His heart was broken because so many had to leave their beloved Trent for a new land, since they were literally dying from hunger. Families could no longer support themselves. There was too little land to feed so many people. The parish priests and bishop celebrated many Masses, and the people who were to make the long and dangerous journey were given words of encouragement and strength.

Vigolo Vattaro was a town of approximately two thousand souls. In a period of 2½ months, 402 people in 19 families left Vigolo Vattaro for Brazil. Each family had many children. Groups of the same family name followed each other.

When Napoleone returned home after six months of working away from his dear family, he had enough money to take his family to Brazil. Amabile, jumping up and down with great excitement, grabbed her father and kissed and hugged him. Amabile was so happy to see her daddy home at last. She asked him, "Papa, do we have enough money to leave for Brazil?" He answered, "Yes, my loved one. My wallet is filled and we are going soon!" "When, Papa?" asked Amabile. "I do not know. We must prepare. You will have to help your mother because there are many things to do. We are going into the forests of America where there are beasts and Indians. We must be prepared." Amabile remembers saying, "Beasts and Indians?" Her father reassured her. "Don't worry, honey, we will take care of everything. We will be welcomed by the Indians. They are not evil. God will protect us and Our Blessed Mother will guide us." Anna said to the children, "We must take our pots and pans, our sheets and blankets, and our dishes and cutlery. The only things we will leave behind are the table and chairs and our beds."

Amabile was full of questions. "Are there churches in America, Papa?" "Are there schools in America?" "Do the Indians know Jesus?" "Do the beasts eat people?"

Her father answered, "Yes, my child, there are churches in Brazil, but where we are going is virgin forest and there are no churches."

Amabile answered, "What a pity! What are we going to do without Our Lord in the Blessed Sacrament?" Her father tried to console her saying, "It is going to be fine. We are going to build our church, and we are going to start new towns. There will be many churches. You will see."

After six months of preparation for the arduous journey, the families were ready. They would be leaving in the evening. There were many tears among the friends, families and neighbors who remained. They were lighting lanterns and crying knowing that this would be the last time they would see each other. Emotions were strong. They would never see their beloved Tyrol again! There were last minute thoughts. "Maybe we should stay." "Maybe things will get better." No. No. They had made their decision, and they were leaving their homeland forever!

The immigration from northern Italy to Brazil was much different than immigration to the United States. In the United States most of the immigrants were destined for the cities, for work in the mines, on the railroads, and in slate and stone quarries. In Brazil, the Trentini would become real pioneers, hacking out farms and towns from the jungle forests of southern Brazil. They would be harassed by Indians, the unfamiliar elements of jungle weather and exotic animals, but they would persevere and grow in wisdom and strength.

Leaving their homeland, the sacred place of their birth, was a traumatic experience for the Vigolani. To leave that mountain, that beautiful valley (Valsugana), was heart wrenching for these immigrants. Not knowing what was before them, but with great expectations, they looked forward to a land of blessed promise.

CHAPTER 2

Arrival In Brazil

On September 25, 1875, Napoleone and Anna Visintainer, with their children and Anna's mother and father,
Giovanni and Domenica Pianezzer and their sons,
departed Vigolo Vattaro. The group was composed of 109
men, women and children. They went to Trent where they
boarded a train for Le Havre, which was the principal port
of northeast France. The immigrants waited one month
before boarding the ship *San Martin* which was headed
for Brazil.

It took six weeks to arrive at the port of Itajai. When
the boat docked, the Trentini were utterly amazed to hear
a voice greeting them in the Italian language. After hearing nothing but French and Portuguese for the entire trip,
it was a blessing to hear their own language. The man
greeting them was an Italian Jesuit missionary, Fr.
Giovanni Cybeo. Father welcomed them as his dear com-
patriots, and he told them that Brazil received them with
open arms. There was a great show of emotion and they
thanked Father for coming to meet them and reassure
them. They were truly certain that God had blessed them
and that they were destined for a rich and full land. If
God so willed, they would begin the great task of building
a new life. No one among them spoke Portuguese, but
in spite of the odds, these Trentini were ready, with the
help of God, to pioneer and settle a new land.

The king of Brazil was encouraging an increase in immigration to colonize the state of Santa Catarina. This province was very difficult to colonize because of the almost impenetrable forests and mountains, and the fear of the natives who were called the *botocudos.* Santa Catarina is geographically located between Paraná on the north and Rio Grande do Sul on the south, the Atlantic Ocean on the east, and Argentina on the west. In 1829, the first colony of Santa Catarina was founded by Germans and a few years later, in 1836, a large group of Trentini and Venetians established the colony of New Italy.

A group of ten German families founded the port town of Itajai in 1860 and about five years later Italians, Swedes, Danes and Poles settled in this port city.

It was at Itajai that the Visintainer family and the Vigolani disembarked and stayed at barracks provided by the Brazilian government. After a week's rest, the men began the journey into the interior of the state of Santa Catarina. We must remember that there were no roads, horses, oxen or other means of transportation. The men had to forge ahead directly into the forests with machete knives, hatchets and handsaws. The government of Brazil provided 1,100 lots to the immigrants and it was up to the men to choose their farm lots and clear the land. They carried no food, but had guns to hunt game, which was abundant.

They were amazed at the different varieties of wild fruits and the various species of edible vegetables which the guide pointed out to them. Two men could hunt game for an hour and feed twenty men for three days. Napoleone marveled at the wild turkeys and fowl of all kinds. One day the hunters shot monkies and a baboon. The guide said their meat would be delicious. As Napoleone looked upon the almost human looking faces of those animals, he was filled with a great pity and vowed from that day he would never eat the flesh of those poor animals.

When the men and older boys left the women and children at the temporary housing in Itajai, they assured them they would return safely and take them to their new homes. The women and children were then transported by wagons to the town of Brusque in the interior, an area closer to their men. After the very difficult journey, many women became discouraged and began expressing their unhappiness and regret. A few babies died and the women were fearful and disconsolate. They had not heard anything from their men and many feared them dead. Many said they wanted to return home. The language barriers, the unfamiliar food, the longing for the presence of their husbands, older sons and brothers were all elements creating agonizing dissatisfaction.

Father Cybeo tried to calm the women, telling them that homesickness was natural. They had clean and adequate shelter, milk for the children and enough food for all. He asked them to be patient and prayerful. The women and children gathered for Mass each day and prayed the rosary three times each day. News finally came to them that their men were fine and healthy, and would soon return to take them to their new homes.

On Christmas Eve of 1876, after six months away from their families, the men returned. All the families went to St. Louis Church in Brusque, and a Holy Mass of Thanksgiving was celebrated for the safe return of their husbands, sons and brothers. This was their first Christmas in Brazil. It was strange to celebrate Christmas in this tropical weather, so different from the snow and ice of the Christmases in the Tyrol.

Most of the men were very anxious to take their families to their new homes. Napoleone, immediately after the holidays, prepared the family for the long and grueling journey. Amabile remembers her daddy saying, "We are going, my dears, to Vigolo." Amabile quickly responded, "Vigolo? Papa, are we going back to Italy?" "No,

Amabile, we are going to Vigolo." "I do not understand, Papa." Napoleone, with a wry smile, said, "My child, Vigolo is the name we have given to our new land. We have baptized it with the name of our hometown in Italy."

The whole family was amazed and Amabile, with her usual enthusiasm, kissed her father and with glee cried out, "See, Momma, isn't Papa wonderful! We *are* going to live in Vigolo!"

Amabile then asked, "Is there a church in Vigolo, Papa?" Her father told her, "Be calm, my child. The church will be built later, after all the houses are finished. Until then, our houses will be our chapels." She asked, "What about Mass, Papa?" He replied, "Mass, Amabile, is far away, but we will call the priest and he will celebrate Mass in our house from time to time, until we build our church." As far as Amabile was concerned, now was the time!

It was a long and treacherous trip from Brusque, a march of thirty miles on foot. Men, women and children, babies in arms and their few precious belongings, clinging to the memories of home. Through the jungle forest they trudged, unaccustomed to the terrible tropical heat, the insects and mosquitos and the deep mud beneath their feet. In spite of the difficulties, they were strong and anxious to reach their new homes. They sang hymns and the folk songs of the Trentini. As the tired group of hardy peasants approached more closely to the promised land, the men said, "Look, ladies, how beautiful the land is! Look at these gigantic trees, and think of what magnificent houses we can build with the wood! There are plenty of delicious, tasty fruits and wild vegetables to eat. Look at how fertile the land is! There will never be hunger again! God has blessed this magic land. We will make a new Italy here, a new Trent!"

As they made their way to Vigolo, Amabile's father said to her, "Amabile, do you want to see something really beautiful?" In the silence of the jungle, there was a tremendous noise and a huge group of parrots appeared. Napoleone caught a very lovely parrot and gave it to Amabile to keep as her pet. He told her that she must care for the parrot and nurture it with love. She asked her father, "Can this parrot talk, Papa?" He answered, "Certainly he can talk, but you will have to teach him to speak Italian! He will learn how to sing and pray."

In the midst of the journey, before nightfall, the men prepared temporary shelter so they could eat and rest. What a feast they enjoyed! There was rabbit, pheasant and all kinds of fruits, berries and vegetables. Surely in this land no one would ever die from hunger.

During the night, there were many frightening noises from the jungle. Amabile said to her father, "Papa, I am afraid! Are there tigers and savages here?" Her father reassured her, "There is no reason to be afraid, dear one. It is just the animals and birds singing us to sleep. Now rest, for tomorrow we have a long trip to our new home." After prayers and hymns, the families rested for the night.

The next day, after traveling on foot, they arrived in a magnificent valley covered in lush vegetation. The mountains reminded them of Vigolo Vattaro in Italy and they rejoiced in the beauty of their new home.

The men had constructed houses of wood covered with straw, but the women were rather anxious and afraid that the straw would not be strong enough to keep out the wind and rain. The house Napoleone built for his family had one large room with palm leaves on the floor and a straw roof. It was very clean and neat. He also made beds from the eucalyptus leaves and instructed his wife and Amabile to put the sheets over the leaves to make comfortable and fragrant beds. In the corner of the huge room, Napoleone had constructed a fireplace. He was an excellent stonemason and had made the fireplace from the native stone. It was at this *focolare* (fireplace) that the family had their first meal. Napoleone hunted and brought home a fat pheasant. Anna prepared it for the first meal in their new home.

The first thing Anna did when they arrived in that rather primitive home was to place a crucifix on the wall and a small statue of Our Blessed Lady on the fireplace shelf. After a wonderful meal, the family prayed the rosary together and sang the *Salve Regina* (Hail Holy Queen). It was the first religious song sung on that tropical night. Echoing in the night were the songs and prayers of the other pioneers in their own homes, accompanied by the birds singing along with them.

After a restful night, the Visintainer family arose and saw the glorious beauty of their surroundings. They also became aware of the tremendous amount of work to be done in the heart of this American forest. When Amabile opened her eyes on that first morning, she heard an orchestra of birds and her parrot singing brightly, as if to say, "Get up Amabile! There's work to be done!"

On their land, they found wild strawberries, lemon trees and orange trees. Since there were no cows or goats, the babies were given coconut milk. Someday they would get cows and mules, but now they had to make do with what they found on the land. Napoleone and his sons had to hunt each day, but the forests were replete with rabbits, turkey and pheasant.

During this time the men were clearing fields and marking off their properties. Soon they would plant *manioca,* which was a root vegetable, like the potato, and very easy to grow in the tropics. They also planted wheat and corn, staple crops for the making of bread and *polenta.*

CHAPTER 3

Settling In

As the family waited for the first crop, many people, knowing of Napoleone's talent as a stonemason, asked him to build permanent stone foundations for their wooden homes. He was also busy constructing permanent fireplaces for each home. The fireplace, known as the *focolare,* was the focal point, the gathering place of the family. Since there was no money, Napoleone was paid for his work in meat and foods such as wild fowl, rabbits, deer, wild berries and fruit.

Stones were abundant in the mountain, creeks, and river of Vigolo. The foundations of the houses were built in stone and then finished in wood by the carpenters. The trees felled by the men in clearing the fields were used as lumber. Napoleone, as a bricklayer, made bricks from mud and a few houses were constructed of brick. Stone fences were used to mark off the fields and meadows of each property owner. In those days, the Visintainer table was always full and abundant. With the first harvest, the Visintainer family enjoyed their first *polenta* and bread. The precious seeds they had brought from Italy bore fruit in tomatoes, peppers, zucchini and tender lettuce.

Amabile's eyes filled with tears of joy when she saw the happiness of her mother and father. After working so hard, now they were enjoying the first fruits of their labor. God had truly blessed this land of Brazil!

Not everyone was content and happy with their new
home as the Visintainer family. Many felt that the life was
too hard in the wilds of Santa Catarina. Some said, "We
are living like animals!" "There are no priests, no doctors, no medicine and no milk for the babies!" The pro-
verbial straw that broke the camel's back was the death
of a baby in the colony. After the burial of the baby, many
women said they were going to beg their husbands to
return to Italy. That night Anna asked Napoleone what
he thought about returning to their homeland. Without
hesitation he said to Anna, "Are you daft, woman? *Porca
miseria!* Return to Italy? Italy is beautiful and good, but
don't babies die in Italy also? We left there to avoid dying
of hunger. We must have courage, my wife. What we need
is trust and confidence in God. We have made the right
decision! We are pioneers and settlers! We shall build
cities and towns, a new Italy, richer and more beautiful
and secure. We cannot go back; we must go forward. Our
sacrifices and sufferings will not be in vain. We are building a future for our children!"

Anna never spoke of returning to Italy again, but a
number of families did return to Italy and to an uncertain
future. There were, however, hundreds of new immigrant
families to take their place.

Unfortunately, the native Americans, the Carijo
Indians, never had a good relationship with the new colonists. Most of the Indians were nomadic hunters and
they feared the guns of the colonists. Amabile regretted
that no one tried to make friends with the Indians. Even
at a young age, she dreamed of converting the Indians
and living in peace with them. Fifty miles away from
Vigolo, there was an uprising of hostile Indians and a
group of Polish and German colonists had their farms
and homes destroyed.

Because of the tragedy, many of the Polish colonists
moved closer to Vigolo. Many intermarried with the Trentini and some of the first religious Sisters of Mother

Pauline were Polish girls.

The new colony of Italian-speaking people had no priest or church, but every few months, Fr. Alberto Gatoni visited Vigolo and the colony of Nova Trento, which was about a mile away. Fr. Gatoni, although the grandson of Italians, spoke only German. He was pastor of the town of Brusque, which was fifty miles away from Vigolo. The majority of the people in Brusque spoke German. His presence became a blessing to the people of Vigolo and Nova Trento. In a short time Father was able to learn enough Italian to give a simple sermon and was able to make himself understood to his flock.

Whenever Fr. Gatoni came to the area he stayed at the home of Napoleone Visintainer. What joy Amabile had in serving the priest and making him comfortable, learning from him the things of God!

The Jesuit Fathers were given the spiritual care of a huge area of the state of Santa Catarina by the Church and government of Brazil. The Jesuits, realizing the need for an Italian-speaking priest, chose Fr. Archangelo Gannerini, a young, zealous, vigorous, and holy priest to take Fr. Gatoni's place. There was great sorrow when Fr. Gatoni was transferred from the parish of Brusque and his many missions, but Fr. Gannerini was a Tyrolean. He understood them. He knew their vices and their virtues. He was truly one of their very own. In spite of the long distance, Fr. Gannerini came from Brusque to the Trentini faithfully, twice a month, to celebrate Mass, baptize the babies, and more frequently, to bury the dead.

Nova Trento was growing much faster than Vigolo, which remained a farming community. In 1876, the Jesuit Fathers held the first mission in Italian at Nova Trento. The priests who preached the week-long mission revival were amazed with the faith and spiritual energy of these colonists of Vigolo and Nova Trento. They urged them to make plans to build their own churches.

Napoleone Visintainer, his sons and some other men set about building the stone and cement chapel which was named St. George in honor of their home parish in Vigolo Vattaro, Italy. The dream of Amabile was fulfilled! At last they had a church! Each evening the colonists went to the chapel for prayers and hymns. On the Sundays when the priest did not come to Vigolo, they recited the rosary and Eucharistic Prayers and sang hymns of praise.

The people of Vigolo now had Jesus in the Blessed Sacrament in their midst. Jesus, the Lord! The Body, Blood, Soul and Divinity of the Divine Saviour with them! Nothing would be impossible for them to accomplish now.

The Vigolani realized the need for a catechetical school to prepare the children for the sacraments and to teach them how to read and write. A small building was constructed next to the chapel at Vigolo to be used primarily to teach the Italian language and catechism. The first teacher at the school was Marina Dallabrida.

Amabile wanted very much to go to school, but because she was the eldest daughter, there were many duties and chores at home. As with many pioneer children, each child had to contribute to the well-being of the farm and family. She knew the alphabet and tried in her free time to learn how to read from her mother's prayerbook which was written by St. Alphonsus and entitled *La Massima Eterna*.

When the time for First Holy Communion approached, Amabile was told she could not receive Holy Communion because she did not know how to read. She was crushed and saddened. The more she tried to learn, the less she remembered.

First Holy Communion would be given at a solemn Mass for the children of all colonists in St. Joseph Chapel in Allianza, which was ¾ of a mile from Vigolo. Only the children who were properly instructed and who had obtained the teacher's recommendation could receive their First Communion. Marina Dallabrida felt very bad that she could not recommend Amabile. Everyone loved Amabile. She was the kind of person who was kind and loving, with a simplicity that charmed young and old. Everyone was praying for her success. Two weeks before the date of Holy Communion, her mother said to the sad Amabile, "We shall pray to the Holy Spirit. The whole family will make a novena to the Holy Spirit that you will learn, at least, to read the basics."

Many friends joined the family in prayer and Amabile persevered each day in trying to read. Lo and behold, three days before Holy Communion, Amabile read to Marina Dallabrida from the book her mother had given her.

Marina Dallabrida was absolutely amazed because Amabile was able to read perfectly.

She exclaimed, "What has happened? What miracle has occurred? Before you could not read. Now you are able to read!"

Amabile exclaimed, "My family and I prayed to the Holy Spirit, and I asked for the gift to read. God is so good to me!"

Marina Dallabrida said she would now recommend Amabile to the priest for her to receive her First Holy Communion. Amabile ran home to tell her mother.

"Mama, I can read! Listen to me read from your book!"

Her mother asked, "How is this possible? Let me hear you!"

Without hesitation Amabile read. The younger children marveled. Her mother kissed and hugged her with tremendous joy, thanking God that her wonderful daughter would be able to receive the Lord Jesus in Holy Communion! Amabile rejoiced that now she could become one with her Jesus in the Most Blessed Sacrament. The whole family immediately began a novena of thanksgiving to the Holy Spirit.

CHAPTER 4

The Life of The Spirit in Vigolo

In 1878, the Jesuit missionaries, for the second time, preached a retreat in Nova Trento. Once again, they were impressed with the faith and spiritual life of the people and decided to establish a Jesuit House in Nova Trento.

The provincial superior of the Jesuits, Fr. Augustus Servanzi, came to live in Nova Trento. With him were Fr. Gian Maria Cybeo and Br. Pietro Cunze. The faithful of the area were absolutely overjoyed to have the priests so close to them.

Fr. Cybeo of Nova Trento was delegated to confer the sacrament of Confirmation upon the people of Vigolo and Nova Trento. Since Amabile and her oldest brother were confirmed in Italy, only her sister Giuseppina was eligible to receive the sacrament.

Amabile's best friend, Virginia Nicolodi, had already received Confirmation. She also had a sister, Fortunata, who would be receiving Confirmation at this time.

Virginia wanted so much to be a part of Amabile's life and to strengthen the bond of friendship that she asked Amabile to be her sister's godmother for Confirmation. In turn, Virginia offered to become the godmother for Amabile's sister, Giuseppina. Amabile thought it was a wonderful idea. Then they would be more than friends; they would become *commare*. The spiritual relationship of *commare* (godmother) and *compari* (godfather) established a bond that lasted a lifetime. Among Italians it has become a way of expressing respect and special love for the person chosen to be godparent. In fact, the members of both families all become relatives.

With the permission of their respective parents, Virginia and Amabile became bound to each other's families at the first Confirmation in the pioneer colony. In fact, the families became very close and later Napoleone Visintainer and Francesco Nicolodi became partners in the first mill of the area.

The completion of the Chapel of St. George and its approaching dedication brought great joy to the people of Vigolo. Fr. Servanzi stayed in the Visintainer home during the days of preparation. The colonists participated in a retreat and assisted at Holy Mass each day. Fr. Servanzi blessed every home and consecrated each family to Jesus and Mary.

During his stay in Vigolo, Fr. Servanzi had come to notice the piety and deep spiritual nature of Amabile and Virginia. He saw in them something very special, even at so young an age. He was profoundly impressed by their wisdom, understanding of faith, and dedication to the things of God.

A few weeks after the retreat and celebration at Vigolo, Fr. Servanzi visited the Visintainer home once more. He wished to speak to Amabile's parents alone, concerning Amabile's future. He felt Amabile had a religious vocation and should be allowed to join a religious community in Rio de Janeiro.

Napoleone was delighted. He thought it was a real blessing from God that his little girl had the gift of a calling to serve the Lord. Anna, his wife, felt otherwise. She said Amabile was immature and too idealistic. She was concerned that Amabile, a country girl, would be unable to cope with a big city especially since she spoke very little Portuguese. She thought it would crush her traumatically to leave home. Anna felt that Fr. Servanzi was pushing her and that he really did not know her well. She was unhesitatingly against the plan.

Amabile could not help hearing the news. She was extremely excited. Her hopes and dreams would be fulfilled! God wanted her for His own. She immediately ran to Virginia's house to share the great news. Virginia wanted to go with her dear friend. Both were so excited. They were going to Rio!

Virginia Nicolodi had been injured at birth and she walked with a pronounced limp. Her parents were very protective of her, and they were adamantly against her leaving home for a religious community so far away. Amabile's mother and Virginia's parents joined forces to convince the girls to wait until they were older and more mature.

Anna said to Amabile, "My daughter, I know what is in your heart. I know how much you want to serve God. To be a Sister in Christ you must be a saint! They have so much to do! I see your holiness and zeal. My child, it is not enough to want to go to Rio. You must know how to read and write Portuguese. Besides, you aren't a city girl. You would be completely lost and unhappy in Rio de Janeiro. Be patient a while longer. I need you so much at home, my Ambiliotta. You are indispensible to me. Without you, I cannot go on. I could not manage with the house and children." Amabile understood this to mean, "This is God's will. I am not ready. My family needs me. Charity and obedience now!"

Twice each week, Fr. Servanzi and Br. Pietro taught catechism in Nova Trento. Amabile and Virginia, with many others, went faithfully to the sessions, which were mainly for teenagers and adults. Fr. Servanzi asked Amabile and Virginia to accept the responsibility of teaching the little children their religion. Then he could concentrate on teaching the adolescents, while Br. Pietro would teach the adults.

Amabile accepted the task with pleasure. This was

another sign for her to devote her life to God's work. Virginia, at first, was upset and very nervous. She said, "How can we poor country girls teach catechism to the little children?" Amabile told her not to be afraid. "We shall be like apostles. Our Lady and St. Joseph will help us to show Jesus to the little children. You and I have been chosen. We must not fear or be timid. We must do what God asks through Fr. Servanzi for the good of the little children who are very close to God. This will be our mission for Christ."

Every morning at 4 a.m. Amabile and Virginia walked to Nova Trento for morning Mass. They must have seemed to others a strange pair as they walked together in the early morning hours before the sun rose, Virginia, limping alongside Amabile's strong stride, praying and singing hymns on their way to Mass.

One day Virginia was sick and unable to go to Mass, so Amabile went alone. On her way home from church a woman approached her along the road and started talking to her. The woman was Italian. She had been living in the provincial capital for 12 years. Her husband had abused her emotionally and physcially, after which he had abandoned her and her three daughters. In order to support themselves, she and the two oldest daughters had gone into prostitution in the city.

As the woman cried, Amabile was overcome with sadness and tried to comfort the poor woman. There was more. The woman said that her two daughters were murdered by men who took advantage of them. Soon after their deaths, the woman took her only daughter and fled from the horrible dangers of the city.

Amabile, with the good sense of a peasant girl, asked the woman if she had come to Nova Trento to start prostitution. "Do you realize what you have done? You have already lost two daughters to sin."

Amabile began to speak of God to the woman. The woman wanted no part of God. She cried, "God didn't feed us in our hunger. Nobody cares. All we have is misery. The only way we could survive was by prostituting ourselves."

Amabile took her crucifix and in a calm and soothing voice said, "My dear, Jesus loves you. Jesus died for you." She put the crucifix close to the woman's eyes and said, "He loves you more now because you need Him so much. You mean more to Him than anyone else because you are one of His lost sheep. He is looking for you. He needs you and wants you near Him. I did not meet you by chance. You are coming with me. We are going to help you. I want to meet your daughter. We are going to find a way that you can live with Jesus and the good people of this area."

The woman was very moved. She took the crucifix and placed it close to her heart and asked, "My child, who are you? Why do you care about me?" Amabile said, "I see Jesus in you. You are a good woman. God has much for you to do."

Amabile took the woman to the priest and they found a good Christian family for her to live and work with. She and her daughter were able to live and work in Nova Trento until they became independent. Her daughter met and married a good man and they all remained faithful to God and His Church. The woman remained in Nova Trento until her death.

The incident of the woman's plight convinced Amabile that she had a mission to help others. She wanted so much to reach out to those in need. How could she do it? What method could she use? When should she begin? She was needed by her own family. Her work was at home. Surely that was her vocation.

CHAPTER 5

God's Will for Amabile

Life for Amabile and her friend, Virginia, centered on Church, home, the farm, and the mill where they ground the corn, wheat and *manioca* grown by their neighbors.

One day her father called all the children together and said, "My children, the sugar cane is ready to be harvested. We must work together to cut it, mash it and make sugar." They began the strenuous and difficult job of making the sugar and syrup for their needs.

At the same time they had to pick the ripe grapes to make wine. After putting the grapes into a huge wooden bin, Amabile's father and brothers would wash their feet very carefully, get into the bin, and stomp the grapes with their bare feet. At the base of the wooden bin was a trough and, as the juice came forth, the other children would funnel it into smaller wooden barrels. The children would beg Napoleone for a taste of the sweet nectar and gleefully Napoleone would ask their opinion of the grape juice. Amabile joyfully took the first cup of juice to her mother, who remained in the house. This was a time of happiness for the family. Their hard work was bearing fruit!

The pioneer family bonded more closely together through the days of work and prayer. Amabile was very close to her sister, Giuseppina, whom she called "Beppina." In her writings, she said, "Beppina is as sweet as wine, so good and kind, my dear sister.''

Amabile and Virginia were tireless in their work for the sick and the poor. Each day they would work in their respective homes, fields, and in the mill. In addition, they joyfully cleaned the chapel, took care of the sanctuary, and taught the catechism to the little children. With all of this work, they found time to help the sick and especially to care for pregnant women and their homes. The poor received their special attention as they begged food for them.

In the village of Vigolo, there was a 12 year old girl who had a mysterious sickness. She would suddenly burst forth in shrill screams, shaking and rocking back and forth. After a few hours, she would become perfectly calm, with no memory of the bizarre behavior. No one knew what caused these outbursts, and her parents were at their wit's end.

Amabile and Virginia tried to help the parents. They befriended the young girl and spent time with her to determine the reason for such odd behavior. Everyone was puzzled. Amabile suggested to Virginia that they should make a novena to the Sacred Heart of Jesus while fasting.

"Jesus will hear us. He loves this family. The poor parents have tried everything. They must join us in prayer.'' Accordingly, Amabile and Virginia, with a simple, uncomplicated faith and unwavering trust, began the novena. Two days after the novena, the young girl stopped having these horrible outbursts and never again was troubled by them.

Frs. Servanzi and Sabattini, from the Jesuit House of Nova Trento, wanted a congregation of Sisters to establish a school in Nova Trento for the daily instruction and education of the children. The state had not provided a school in the colony, and there was no financial help forthcoming.

When Amabile and Virginia heard of the plan, they promised God that they would enter the convent of the

Sisters who would come to Nova Trento. The two girls already lived like religious Sisters. They went to Mass each day, made their meditation and spiritual reading every day and, with great intensity, they abstained from meat and fasted four days a week. With all their hard work, they continued to fast.

Days, weeks, months passed—still no Sisters. One day Fr. Servanzi was a guest at dinner in the Visintainer home. During the meal, Father, with much sadness, said that Sisters would not be coming to Nova Trento. There were no Sisters available, and the superiors of the Jesuits in Rio de Janeiro felt that supporting a community of nuns in Nova Trento was impossible. A school and convent must be built and maintained, but the colonists were too poor for this expensive project.

Amabile repeated the conversation to Virginia. The two girls were filled with agony. Their hopes were dashed again. They would never have the chance of becoming religious Sisters. What would they do? Was there any other way?

About two weeks after the devastating news, Amabile said to Virginia, "I think we should build a little house next to the Chapel of St. George. We could both live together as Sisters. We would pray and help the sick, teach catechism and be of assistance to anyone in need."

Virginia thought it was a great idea, yet she had some questions. How could they build a house? Their parents would never allow them to live there alone. She discussed these thoughts with Amabile.

"Don't worry, Virginia. God will take care of it. This is His will. I'll talk to Fr. DeAngeli. He is young and will understand." Fr. DeAngeli was one of the staff of missionaries at the Jesuit House in Nova Trento. Amabile spoke to Fr. DeAngeli, but the first thing he said was for them to get their parents' permission. Napoleone was not opposed to the idea, but Anna absolutely refused. She thought it was a stupid idea and said to Amabile, "What is in your head to leave this house and take poor, sick Virginia with you? Charity begins at home. Don't you see how these children need you? You are a dreamer. I know very well you want to be a nun, but you must be realistic. You have fantasies and delusions! Forget them. Living in a shack near the church is unreasonable. Settle down to earth. You are needed here. This is your chapel—at home with your family."

Napoleone tried to soothe Amabile by telling her that her mother was pregnant and sick. She was upset because her Amabilotta wanted to leave home. Amabile had always been close to her dear mother, and she certainly understood her feelings of love and concern.

In spite of the opposition from Amabile's mother and Virginia's parents, the pioneer girls intensified their sacrifices and mortifications, praying for a way to serve God as His chosen spouses.

A few months later, tragedy struck the Visintainer home. On the 7th day of August, 1886, after 24 hours of tremendous suffering, Anna died with the child in her womb. This loving mother and wife, this pioneer heroine, this martyr, gave her life for her family. Amabile was at one side of her bed and Napoleone at the other. She was so weak that she was unable to speak. Before she died, she took from her neck the cross she had worn since her wedding day and gave it to Amabile. She said, "My sweet child, take care of your father and brothers and sisters." Turning to her husband, she said, "Take care of our children!" Then closing her eyes, she cried, *"Gesu, Misericordia!"* ("Jesus, have mercy!") Anna was 47 years of age.

Amabile realized at the moment of her mother's death that, in God's plan, she was to become the mother of the family. With her face bathed in tears, Amabile washed her mother's body and prepared her for burial. She organized the children to view their dear mother. She sent for the priest and called the neighbors.

Her father was in a daze. He couldn't cry or speak.
It seemed as if he were paralyzed, numbed with grief. He
had lost his dear wife and the child she carried. His mind
was filled with apprehension and his heart overwhelmed
with sorrow. What would happen to his family? There
were 13 children and the youngest was only four years old.
Amabile realized that her dad was unable to cope with
this tragedy. Perhaps he needed time to heal. So she took
over the household to give him time to grieve. Amabile
was 20 years old when her mother died.

The day after her mother's burial, while meditating
before Holy Mass, Amabile knew her dream of becoming
a religious Sister was farther away than ever. "My God,
I don't understand. I don't know your plan for me. Please
help me to see your good purpose in all of this sorrow."

CHAPTER 6

The Call To Mission

Life in the Visintainer home, after Anna's death, was very sad. Napoleone could not find peace and consolation. He could not come to terms with the death of his wife. The entire burden of the family was upon Amabile and Ernest. The boys operated the farm and Amabile the house. They could not reach their father emotionally or spiritually.

One day he said to Amabile, "You must take care of your brothers and sisters. I am going away."

"You are going away?" she cried. "Where are you going?"

He answered that he was going to Nova Trento because they needed a stonemason there. He said he would be home each weekend, but he felt he could no longer keep his sanity. He missed his wife so much he had to get out for a time. He seemed to blame himself for her death. She had worked too hard. Maybe if they had stayed in Italy, this would not have happened. He was filled with regrets and unanswerable questions.

Napoleone, nervous and irritable, went to work building stores, houses, etc. in the growing Nova Trento. He came home each week, but there seemed to be little change in him. To the children he appeared to be always agitated and upset. Amabile worried about him and prayed unceasingly for him.

29

One night, after a long, hard day, as Amabile lay sleeping soundly, she had an extraordinary dream. She was awakened in the dream by enchantingly beautiful music. She looked out of her bedroom window and saw a great white mansion drenched in sunlight. The house had two stories with a grand staircase in front.

Amabile was drawn to the stairs, and as she climbed to the top story, she entered a vast hall which had two thrones. One seat was empty. The other was occupied by a young woman. She was splendidly clad in a bright white tunic with a belt of sky blue and surrounded with a mountain of white flowers.

Amabile believed that the woman was the mistress of the house, but she looked like a picture of the Madonna of Lourdes. Standing next to the lady was a little girl who seemed to accompany her. The little girl beckoned Amabile to come closer because the lady had something very important to say to her.

The woman spoke, but Amabile could not hear her. She got down on her knees to kiss the feet of the woman, but the vision was so dazzlingly bright that she was unable to look at her. Amabile could not understand, so she turned and ran away.

On the next consecutive night, Amabile had the same dream. The lady seemed full of joy and warmth as Amabile, with greater courage, approached the throne. The woman said, "I have a great desire that someday you will do the work of my beloved Son, the salvation of my children."

In the dream, Amabile responded to the lady saying, "How can I do this, my Lady? I am nothing but an ignorant and unlearned child. I know so little about the world, and I must care for my family." Amabile awoke pondering the dream, troubled by the request.

On the third night, the same dream occurred. The lady asked Amabile, "My daughter, what have you decided?"

"I want to obey, my Lady, but I am a nobody. I have nothing. I do not know how to read or write very well."

After saying this, Amabile began to weep.

The lady comforted Amabile and in a soothing voice said, "Child, do not be afraid. I will get you a person to help you begin the work I want."

Immediately a man appeared to the right of the lady. He was dressed in the cassock of a priest. The man appeared full of joy as he came near the woman. The lady, pointing to the man said, "Here is the person who will help you, my child. He will put you on the right path and show you the way in which I want you to work and live."

Amabile told Fr. Servanzi about the dreams. He said it was quite obvious that Our Blessed Lady wanted Amabile to continue her apostolic work among the people. The dream was an affirmation of the work she and Virginia were doing.

Shortly after telling Fr. Servanzi about her dream, Amabile and Virginia received the terrible news that Fr. Servanzi was to be transferred to another mission. After eight years in their midst, Father was to go and work in the Mission of Goyas, hundreds of miles away from them. Both girls were filled with tears and apprehension. What would become of them and their work?

Fr. Angelo Sabatini came to replace Fr. Servanzi. He was a much older man with a rigid, severe manner, but he was a man of great sympathy. Amabile saw his caring nature when she told him of a destitute family living in physical and moral misery. The mother was paralyzed, the father was a drunkard, and the children were neglected.

Fr. Sabatini visited the family each day, and with Amabile and Virginia, took food to the four children. He even joined the girls in washing the family's clothes and cleaning the house.

The new priest did not stay very long in the Mission of Nova Trento. Because of his age and very hard work at Vigolo and Nova Trento, he was transferred to another mission.

The priest who succeeded Fr. Sabatini was Fr. Marcello Rocchi. Fr. Rocchi was known as an apostle with a great devotion to Our Lady of Lourdes. He was a preacher of high regard among Italian speaking people in Brazil.

The moment Amabile saw him, she was stunned, for this was the priest in her dream! He was the very man to whom Our Lady had pointed when she said, "This is the person who will help you."

Fr. Rocchi had great plans for the parish. He formed "The Society of the Children of Mary" and made Amabile and Virginia the directors. With the girls in charge the society grew. The young people formed choirs, honored the Blessed Mother with elaborate processions, and studied their faith. They were involved in many acts of charity for the whole Christian community.

Many people in Vigolo and Nova Trento saw how Fr. Rocchi trained and directed Amabile and Virginia. They feared that perhaps these young women would be taken away from them and sent to the city to become religious Sisters. But their destiny was to remain among their own people. In God's plan they would become religious Sisters, but in their own town and village.

Fr. Rocchi's devotion to Our Lady of Lourdes spurred him to plan the building of a grotto in the church at Vigolo and to place a statue of Our Lady of Lourdes in the grotto. Since there were no funds for such a project, his dream had to be shelved.

Upon hearing of Fr. Rocchi's dream of a grotto, Amabile went to Virginia and said, "Let us cultivate a field of *manioca,* and after harvesting it, we will get enough money to buy a statue of Our Lady of Lourdes."

Virginia said, "We have a field, but who will help us? We can't do it by ourselves."

Amabile, as usual, said, "Don't worry. We'll get help. It won't be a problem."

Everything was arranged. Fr. Rocchi blessed the field and they said many prayers for an abundant crop. All the young people helped to hoe and weed. God truly blessed the *manioca* field and they had a marvelous harvest.

The young men gathered rocks from the nearby mountain for the building of the grotto in the sanctuary of St. George in Vigolo. Fr. Rocchi went to Rio de Janeiro to buy the statue of Our Lady of Lourdes when everything was ready. The beautiful statue of Our Lady was placed in the grotto and the Church of St. George was transformed.

CHAPTER 7

The Dream Fulfilled

Amabile's father, Napoleone Visintainer, was extremely disconsolate over the death of his wife, and many people urged him to marry again. They said that Amabile should not be burdened with the role of both mother and father while he lived away from his children. Even though he loved his family and returned to them once a week, he was only a part-time father.

There was a widow named Maria Zamboni. She was a fine young woman who was childless. Everyone knew her to be holy and kind. Napoleone's friends introduced him to her and in the Providence of God, they eventually married.

Amabile was delighted when she met this wonderful woman. According to Amabile, God had solved two problems. Her dear brothers and sisters had a new and loving mother, and her father seemed to be himself once again. Maria Zamboni helped to heal her father's broken heart and made them a complete family.

The realization of Amabile's desire to become a religious was now much closer. With the marriage of her father, she was free to fulfill the request Our Lady had made in her dream. Maybe now was the time to seek the opportunity to serve God in a special way. "Show me the way, Lord," she prayed.

Fr. Rocchi heard about a poor abandoned woman from

the Tyrol. She had immigrated to Nova Trento and had raised her family. After the death of her husband, she became sick from cancer. Her daughters had married and moved from the area. Alone and unable to care for herself, she had no means of support. She was homeless and suffering.

When Fr. Rocchi decided to help this poor woman, there was no one to take her into their home. In order to resolve this situation, Fr. Rocchi and his two diligent nurses, Amabile and Virginia, devised a plan.

Near the Chapel of St. George, in Vigolo, beyond the new Grotto of Our Lady of Lourdes, was a little hut owned by a Baron Beniamino Gaiotti. Father asked the Baron if he could have the dilapidated shack for a hospital infirmary. The Baron gave the little hut to Father and told him to use it as he wished.

The hut was blessed by Fr. Rocchi, and he "christened" it the Little Hospital of St. Vigilio, on June 26, 1890, the Feast Day of St. Vigilio, Patron Saint of Trento, Italy. Amabile and Virginia would direct the hospital, and the poor, cancerous woman was their first patient.

While the two girls readied the hut by cleaning and washing every inch of the building, Napoleone and his sons made the necessary repairs and moved in a bed, small table, and a cabinet. Amabile had a variety of folk medicines, healing herbs and syrups which she placed in the cabinet of the hut.

Amabile and Virginia told their respective parents that it was necessary for them to live in the Little Hospital if they were to give proper care to the cancerous woman. Their families were adamant in their refusal. Father Rocchi begged the parents to give permission, because if the plan was going to work, they must live in the infirmary. Virginia's parents were very worried, especially since she was rather frail and not as strong as Amabile. The girls would have to sleep on the floor and be without the comforts of their homes. The chapel was rather isolated from other homes and the hut would be unprotected.

After much prayer and persistence by the girls and Fr. Rocchi, the parents gave their permission for them to stay at the hut. When the cancer patient arrived, they cleaned her and anointed her body. The stench was terrible and Napoleone asked his daughter how they were going to live in the same room as this woman. Virginia and Amabile were so happy that they were doing God's work they did not mind the awful odor. They began a common life of prayer, work, and suffering.

The cancerous woman was not a tender, loving woman. She was constantly yelling, cursing and screaming at them. The girls understood that it was the pain that caused her behavior. They prayed that God would calm her and give her an opportunity to open her heart to Jesus.

Many of the people from Vigolo were delighted with the infirmary, and they took their babies and children to them for remedies and help. It was amazing that these country girls had such a wide knowledge of folk medicine.

About a month after the blessing of the hut, a horrible incident occurred. Some dirty-minded young men came to the Little Hospital while Amabile and Virginia were sleeping. They yelled obscenities and called them witches. They did not physically harm the girls, but gave them a bad scare.

Napoleone was furious when he heard of this attack on the girls. He told Fr. Rocchi that the girls could no longer remain at the Little Hospital. He would not allow his daughter and Virginia to be frightened and hurt by anyone.

Fr. Rocchi agreed that it was dangerous for the two young girls to remain in the hut. Napoleone owned a two room cabin on his farm. It was decided that the woman patient and the girls would come to live there immediately. Taking a cart pulled by an ox, Napoleone and Luigi brought the contents of the hut, the patient, and the girls to their new little hospital.

Having a two room cabin was a great luxury for the girls. The sick woman had her own room, and the other room was the dispensary and bedroom for the girls. They cooked and washed outside the cabin. The first thing they did was hang a picture of St. Joseph on the wall. Fr. Rocchi blessed the picture and asked St. Joseph to protect their new home. They settled in and began receiving patients.

One day as Napoleone visited the cabin, he noticed that there was very little food. He asked the girls what they had been eating. They replied that they had sufficient food, but they were doing penance for sins and mortifying themselves for the love of God. They had been praying late into the night and sleeping on the floor without linens or even a coverlet.

Napoleone and Virginia's parents became upset at the lifestyle of the girls and went to Fr. Rocchi. Napoleone said he could not stand by and watch his daughter live this way. He would force her to return home and live a sane life.

Fr. Rocchi scolded the girls for their excessive and rigorous mortification. He told them it was not necessary to go to extremes. They had to keep up their strength and health. God needed them to do this work among the people. Amabile and Virginia reluctantly obeyed and mitigated their penances.

The work of the devil continued against the girls when Napoleone and his sons went away for a few days. The same group of young hooligans came to the cabin and began singing immoral songs and making obscene gestures. As they taunted the girls with cries of evil, Amabile yelled, "Get out of here! Leave us alone!" Both girls were extremely frightened and they knelt helplessly before the picture of St. Joseph praying for courage. After a few hours of tormenting the girls with evil suggestions and impure threats, they left.

When Napoleone and his sons, Ernesto and Luigi, heard of this incident, they told the girls they could not continue to stay in the cabin. The cabin was too far from the family house and the family. Napoleone had never reconciled himself to the fact that Amabile wanted to do this work. He was very unhappy because he did not approve of the extreme poverty in which Amabile and Virginia lived. Besides, he suffered from the loss of her presence at home. With a determined resolve, he went to tell her to come back home.

He said, "My child, leave this foolishness. You will die of starvation. You give the food that you have to the people who come to the hospital. This is crazy! You and Virginia have a good home to go to. Please listen and come home!"

Amabile said, "Daddy, please do not worry. We are fine. There is no need to fret."

"Can't you see that the life you are leading here is not human? It is the life of a dog. It is a shame for me to see you living this way," continued Napoleone.

Finally Amabile retorted, "Daddy, that is the devil talking! Please let me be in peace. This is the way we want to live. Do not be afraid, Daddy. I am happy. Do not think I am suffering. I am joyful to be doing what God wants me to do. Please believe me, Daddy. I love this life!"

Napoleone had no choice but to look into his daughter's beautiful face and realize that nothing in this world would change her mind.

Fr. Rocchi was aware of Napoleone's attitude toward Amabile and Virginia. He knew he was disgruntled and upset with the way of life they had chosen. So Father and many parishioners went to speak to him of the wonderful work the girls were doing for the whole community.

"The real truth, Father, is that I am sorrowful and cannot be happy about this situation. I know she is moved by charity, but she is my daughter and it hurts me to see her live this way."

Knowing Napoleone's pride, Fr. Rocchi said, "If you want to help your daughter, donate a plot of land to the Little Hospital of St. Vigilio and we can plant it. The girls can use whatever money they make from the harvest to help them live a better life."

Napoleone was delighted with the idea. He and his children, with Amabile and Virginia, planted a field and a garden with all kinds of vegetables for their needs. Amabile's brothers also built a covered courtyard near the hospital where the girls taught catechism to the little children. They also taught the older girls to cook, sew, and repair shoes.

Taking matters into their own hands, Amabile's brothers and father hid each evening in the woods near the cabin waiting for another attack by the hoodlums. Sure enough, one evening the boys returned to harass Amabile and Virginia. Napoleone and his sons gave them a sound trouncing, and after a spectacular fight, the hooligans ran away as the cowards they were. They didn't disturb the girls again.

Their woman patient who had cancer became gravely ill. Her personality, however, changed from a cantankerous, complaining, cynical person to a calm, gentle, loving Christian. The prayers of Amabile and Virginia had been answered. God's grace flooded the soul of the woman. She began to pray with the girls, thanking God for their heroic patience. The woman said, "Amabile, you are from Heaven. God gave you to me. Dear Virginia, pardon me for my rudeness. I love you. Forgive me for the times I have hurt you." The woman went to Confession, opened her heart to Jesus in Holy Communion, and died a holy death.

Maria, Napoleone's second wife, said to him, "Now that the cancerous woman has died, surely Amabile will come back home." Napoleone agreed.

But Amabile and Virginia had no intention of going home to their parents. Their work had just begun! In fact, Amabile told Virginia that now they would have more time to pray in silent recollection and perhaps have a retreat.

Virginia asked Amabile who would be the spiritual director for their retreat. Without hesitation, Amabile told her, "Father Rocchi, of course!"

Fr. Rocchi gave the girls the Spiritual Exercises of St. Ignatius, used by the Jesuits, and a book by Fr. Frassinetti, called *The Religious at Home*. They began the retreat with a novena of preparation for the feast day of Our Lady of the Holy Rosary. They closed the hospital for eight days during the retreat, slept for three hours a night, and ate frugally. After the retreat, Fr. Rocchi gave the two girls the 38 rules of the spiritual life of the Jesuits.

CHAPTER 8

Benefactors of God's Work

Shortly after the retreat, Virginia became very ill. She had a fever and suffered exhaustion. After a few days of rest and nourishment, she bounced back as energetic as ever. Once again, Fr. Rocchi had to caution the girls to eat well and get enough rest.

However, the spiritual life of the two girls was always intense and sometimes accompanied by imprudent mortification; yet, their apostolate continued with a great amount of spiritual fruit.

A few months after Virginia's illness, Amabile became very ill. The sickness began with severe pains in the abdomen and stomach, followed by an extremely high fever. She was so weak she was unable to stand. Whenever she would try the slightest exertion, she would faint. In a week the pain extended throughout her body and left her practically paralyzed.

Napoleone feared for his daughter's life and he decided to bring her home. In her weakened condition, Amabile protested. However, when her father insisted that she see a doctor, she agreed. Her father took her to Itajai and she was seen by two doctors. Both doctors informed Amabile that nothing could be done for her because of a stomach tumor. Napoleone was shattered. No one could help his beloved daughter.

On the return trip to Vigolo, Amabile was in terrible

pain, but she begged to be taken back to the Little Hospital where Virginia would take care of her. Amabile became so ill on her return trip that she lost consciousness. Her father began planning for her funeral. He called Fr. Rocchi to minister the Last Rites. Virginia stayed by her side praying, ministering to her, and trying to give her comfort.

At daybreak, on the fourth day of the coma, she opened her eyes. Virginia leaned over her with joy and said, "Amabile, how do you feel? We thought you might be dead. How frightened we were to see you so helpless."

Amabile smiled and said, "No, I am not dead. The pain seems to be gone, but I feel so weak. May I have some water?"

As the day progressed, Amabile seemed to get stronger. Everyone was jubilant. Napoleone said it was truly a miracle because the doctors had said she could not be helped and would most probably die.

Amabile told Virginia of the dream she had while unconscious. "There was a great plain with trees and beautiful flowers. Groups of children, dressed in white, sang and walked around the plain. In the midst of the field was a long staircase that extended up to the skies. On the first step of the staircase was Our Blessed Mother who said, 'Here are the daughters that I commit to you.' Then Our Lady came forward to me and took my hand as she led me up the staircase."

Years later, many of the same girls Amabile had seen in her dream would become Sisters in her congregation. After the dream, Amabile felt great joy and an overwhelming peace. She knew she would get well, for she had work to do for Our Mother. Her recovery took only a few days. Then she dedicated herself to preparing twenty little girls for their First Holy Communion.

Many people of Vigolo and the surrounding area began to refer to Virginia and Amabile as "our little nurses." Older girls began to be attracted to the life of the Little Hospital.

The first young lady to join Amabile and Virginia was Theresa Maoli. She was 29 years of age. She was born in the Tyrol in the village of Cles and emigrated with her family to Brazil. On the feast of the Birth of Our Lady, September 8, 1891, Theresa went to live with Amabile and Virginia. Now there were three!

A little more than a year later, Fr. Guiseppe Montero, superior of the Jesuits in Brazil, made a canonical visit to the Jesuit residence in Nova Trento. During the visit, Fr. Rocchi took him to the Little Hospital of Vigolo and introduced him to the three nurses. Fr. Montero was tremendously impressed with the girls and their work.

The Jesuit superior told Fr. Rocchi that the girls needed more room to live decently and a more spacious area to treat the sick. Fr. Montero also discussed with the other priests the possibility of moving the hospital to Nova Trento, which was a larger town as well as the county center. There were few people in Vigolo. In Nova Trento the apostolate would be much larger. Since there was no hospital in Nova Trento, and many people there were in need of help, the superior was confident that benefactors and patrons could be found to support this plan. Amabile's family and the others girls' families were jubilant at the thought of their loved ones leaving the cramped quarters of the Little Hospital.

Amabile had many other dreams. She constantly prayed for a school in Nova Trento. Although she already had catechism lessons for the children, and sewing and cooking lessons for the young girls, she wanted a school where all the children could learn to read and write, especially in their adopted language of Portuguese. Most of the people of the area were still speaking the Italian language and the Tyrolean dialects. Many young people were being taught to read and write Italian by their parents and relatives. Very few knew Portuguese, the language of Brazil. For now, Amabile could only dream because there was no money or competent personnel for such an undertaking.

She did not say very much, but kept these ideas in her mind and heart.

Fr. Rocchi and the superior approached a good Christian man, Giovanni Valli, about donating some land that he owned near the parish Church of the Sacred Heart in Nova Trento. Mr. Valli knew of the wonderful work of the Little Hospital in Vigolo, so he offered both the land and the means to build a new infirmary.

Giovanni Valli was a good and generous man. In the early days of the congregation, he was a wonderful benefactor. Being a man of some means, he unhesitatingly gave of himself to the building of the new hospital and residence.

The people of Vigolo objected to the girls moving to Nova Trento because they needed them in their own town. Many people wanted to force them to remain. They blamed the priests and superior for taking the girls from them.

Giovanni, with the help of Napoleone and the carpenters, built a room for the nurses, a dispensary, and rooms for patients. The crowning glory of the new hospital was the chapel.

Fr. Rocchi directed the people of Vigolo to pray a novena in honor of Our Lady of Lourdes to request the safe transferal of the girls to their new home in Nova Trento. Even though many of the people of Vigolo lamented the girls leaving Vigolo, they had a sense of pride that their "Sisters of Charity," as they called them, would be serving the prestigious people of the city.

Amabile did not want to close the Little Hospital of Vigolo, so she asked her friend and helper, Madeline Ogliari, to stay in Vigolo and take care of the Chapel of St. George and the Little Hospital.

About a year later, in February, 1894, Amabile was told that their new house was ready. Because of the opposition of some people, she chose to leave at 2:00 a.m. when all was quiet and everyone was asleep. The girls left with a lantern to light their way, singing hymns and praising God as they walked to Nova Trento carrying their few belongings.

The new hospital was small, but to the girls, after living in a hut for so many years, it was a veritable palace. They were overjoyed to live but a few steps from the parish Church of the Sacred Heart where Holy Mass was available every day!

The central source of strength for the young girls was the Lord Jesus in the Blessed Sacrament. Each day they could be found in church making their Holy Hour.

Many sick came to the hospital, and the girls made innumerable visits to the homes of the sick and handicapped. Sinners were converted to Jesus Christ and the young were gathered together for catechism and prayer. Amabile began to dream of an orphanage for the many children who had lost their fathers and mothers to the harsh rigors of colonial life.

Fr. Rocchi wanted the young nurses to have some formal education in order to live and function in a Portuguese speaking society. He went to a teacher in the newly formed public school and asked his help. The teacher, Mr. Vigilio Fantini, was a devout Catholic and agreed to teach the young nurses without a fee. He had been impressed with their work and wanted to assist them.

Another young woman, Virginia Cestari, joined the three girls in order to share in the ministry and apostolate which would eventually lead to a new religious congregation. Now there were four!

The nurses, as they were called by the people, began each day with Holy Mass and meditation. Jesus in the Holy Eucharist sustained them and gave them strength for their ministry. "All for Jesus and all for our brethren" became Amabile's challenge to her helpers.

As more and more people came to the hospital and

great numbers of children came for instruction, the four young ladies were barraged with requests for food and clothing. Amabile formed a group of young people called the "Society of the Children of Mary" who aided the parish and the nurses in the many needs of the community.

When the needs of the community became too great, she went to Fr. Rocchi and asked permission to cultivate the land which her father had given her so that they would have food for the children and those patients who remained at the hospital.

CHAPTER 9

Crisis and Change

About a year later, on February 4, 1895, Amabile
received a terrible blow. Fr. Rocchi announced that he was
going to be transferred to a new assignment within a
month. Another Jesuit missionary was to take his place.

Amabile and her friends were heartbroken. Who would
take Fr. Rocchi's place? Would their apostolate remain
secure? Would the grand dream end now? After evening
prayers on the same day as the announcement, Amabile
was very worried and upset. She fell into a fitful sleep
after promising Jesus that she would trust in Him and
do the will of the Father in all things.

During the night, Amabile had a dream. In the dream,
she saw Fr. Rocchi talking to another Jesuit missionary.
Fr. Rocchi turned to Amabile and pointing to his companion said, "In God's holy and divine Providence, this is
the priest selected and sent to guide you. Obey him in all
things."

Amabile told the dream only to Virginia, who said,
"They are nothing but dreams, Amabile. Don't put too
much stock in them."

A few weeks after the dream, the new superior of the
Nova Trento Mission arrived. His name was Fr. Louis
Maria Rossi. He was born of a noble family in Romagna,
Italy. Fr. Rossi was one of 20 children. The family was

47

blessed with many religious vocations.

Amabile saw Fr. Rossi for the first time at Mass when Fr. Rocchi introduced him to the people of the parish. Amabile gasped with surprise and recognition. He was the same priest she had seen in her dream!

Amabile wanted to speak to Fr. Rossi about their future, but she felt timid and was only able to say to him, "Praised be Jesus Christ! Good morning, Father." Little did she know that Fr. Rossi would one day be honored with her as co-founder of the Little Sisters of the Immaculate Conception.

After many tearful farewells, Fr. Rocchi departed Nova Trento on March 2, 1895.

A few days later, Fr. Rossi approached Amabile after Mass and said to her, "I see you and the other three girls at Mass every day. Do you live near here?"

Amabile answered, "Yes, Father, we have been living together in a nearby house which we use as a hospital to help the sick. We also teach catechism to the young children."

Fr. Rossi said that he had come to devote himself to all the people, and he was open to their ministry of service. He told Amabile that he would assist them in their needs whenever he could. He said nothing more. Fr. Rossi was a man of few words.

Later he confided that the country girls, wearing their aprons, and their kerchiefs tied around their heads, made a tremendous impression upon him. Fr. Rocchi had told him of these young women, and his first thought had been, "With all the burdens of Nova Trento, I have this group to contend with!" Within a few weeks, however, Fr. Rossi came to see these young women as a blessing to his ministry and to the community of Nova Trento.

About a month after Fr. Rossi's meeting with Amabile, she decided to visit Fr. Rossi with the other three girls and make known their intentions. They wanted to be religious Sisters and take a habit and a rule of life.

Fr. Rossi was familiar with the demands of a religious commitment. He asked the young women to go slowly. He wanted to observe them and their work more closely. He wanted to see the effect of their work upon the people of Nova Trento and Vigolo and the spiritual fruit among them.

Fr. Rossi had received a book concerning the 38 rules of religious life from his sister, who was the Abbess of the Monastery of Corpus Domini in Forli, Italy. He gave this book to the girls and said, "You must now try to live these rules while you are working in your ministry because you will be an active community and not cloistered Sisters. You will be living in the world with Christ and you will be working among your brothers and sisters as Jesus did. As Jesus lived among people, so will you be walking among people. As Our Blessed Mother Mary helps us all, so will you be like her. You will be her daughters."

Fr. Rossi would give them spiritual talks, encourage them, and dedicate them to God. He called them his little Sisters. He urged them by saying, "My little Sisters, put yourselves always in a state of prayer. Whatever you do, do it in and for the Holy Name of Jesus, our Saviour."

One bright day after morning Mass, Fr. Rossi asked Amabile to come to the parish rectory. She was filled with anxiety and wondered what he wanted. As he began speaking, she listened attentively at first and then with growing awe.

A new diocese had been formed from the territory of the Archdiocese of Rio de Janeiro. Nova Trento was now in the Diocese of Curitiba which encompassed the states of Paraná and Santa Catarina.

The bishop of the new diocese was Bishop Joseph Camargo Barros, a former student of Fr. Rossi when Father taught at the Jesuit College of Itu, Brazil. In five months, the new Bishop was to make a pastoral visit to Nova Trento.

Amabile was jubilant because Fr. Rossi told her that he had written to the bishop about the little community. The bishop had responded that he was anxious to see the little Sisters and to speak with Amabile.

The small group was ecstatic! Finally, the turning point had been reached. This was a new beginning. "Our Blessed Mother was right! She is showing us the way," said Amabile. They were vibrant with joy and happiness. Fr. Rossi wanted them to say special prayers for the success of the pastoral visit and to ask for the intercession of St. Joseph.

In order to express her thoughts more fully and completely, Amabile asked her little group to jointly write a letter to St. Joseph. In the letter they told him they wanted him to guide and protect them as he protected the Holy Family. They told him of their hopes for their small community. They wanted him to be their father and intercede for them before the Holy Trinity so that they could become religious Sisters.

After writing the letter, they put it behind St. Joseph's picture, praying each day for a successful pastoral visit by the bishop.

Five months passed. On August 17, 1895, the new bishop arrived in Nova Trento. With great fanfare many people, priests, and dignitaries of state welcomed the bishop. There was a band on hand for the occasion. Preparations were made for a great feast.

During his visit, the bishop was delighted and amazed at the profound faith of these frontier people. He was amazed at the vibrant religious spirit of Nova Trento and Vigolo.

Bishop Barros visited the little community of young women. He spoke to the young ladies and asked each one of them why she wanted to serve God as a religious Sister. He was deeply impressed with this humble band of devoted girls. There is no record of what was said, but

Fr. Rossi tells us in his writings that even though the bishop was tremendously impressed with the girls, he had reservations about them.

Many religious groups had been started in Brazil, but most of them had fallen apart and failed. He was cautious, yet there was something different about these girls. His intuition was that perhaps this group would last.

Before the bishop left Nova Trento, he made an unannounced visit to the little hospital. When he arrived he found the girls on their knees in prayer. He said he had the impression of profound angelic humility. Actually, the bishop was moved by the simplicity, the poverty and the intensity of love in which the young ladies lived.

As he began his journey back to Curitiba, Bishop Barros said to Fr. Rossi, "I shall do everything in my power to document these young ladies as a new religious community. Your Reverence has all the canonical faculties to guide this fledgling group. At an opportune time, you may hear their vows and may call them Sisters. You can also help them choose a religious habit for their new congregation."

Not all of the clergy were enthusiastic about the bishop's decision. Some felt he did not know what he was doing. There was one Jesuit priest, Fr. Parisi, who said it was ridiculous to approve a group of almost illiterate country girls. They were peasant girls without education. How could the bishop be a part of such foolishness? It is now most apparent that the bishop was inspired by the Holy Spirit.

The people of Nova Trento and Vigolo were very excited and happy that a native religious community was being formed from their very own girls.

A few of the older immigrants had a vague recollection of what a nun looked like, but the majority of the people, especially the young, knew nothing about women religious. The only women religious in Brazil were in the cities and large towns far from the pioneer frontier.

After three centuries, the Church in Brazil was about to come of age. It was an exciting time for the Catholics of this great land. Emigrants from Portugal, Spain, Italy, Austria and Germany continued to flock to Brazil. There were also a number of Slavic people, including Poles, Slovaks, and Czechs, who arrived in Brazil from 1890 to 1915. The vast majority of these people were Roman Catholic.

CHAPTER 10

Pioneer Women Become Religious Sisters

Bishop Joseph Camargo Barros gave his formal approbation to the new community on August 25, 1895, about five years after Amabile and Virginia had first moved into the Little Hospital. Amabile was now almost 30 years old.

Professor Vigilio Fantini, who remained the tutor for the young women, was amazed at the growth of the intellectual proficiency in Amabile and her Sisters. With his help, they decided to write a particular rule of life for their new congregation.

Amabile wrote to the Abbess Maria Angelica, Fr. Rossi's sister, asking for her assistance in writing a rule of life for an active community. The abbess responded with wisdom, and inspired Amabile and the young girls to work with Fr. Rossi and Professor Fantini in writing their rule.

The young ladies took to the task of learning to read and understand the many theological books "as ducks take to water," said Professor Fantini. He wrote of their progress and almost miraculous comprehension of diffi-cult concepts.

Fr. Rossi and the bishop felt that since Amabile, Virginia and Theresa had been living, working and praying together as a community, it was not necessary to have a period of canonical postulancy. It was decided that they should have a novitiate lasting four months.

During this period as novices, Amabile, Virginia and Theresa entered into a spirit of meditative silence, study and physical work, with private and communal prayer. Fr. Rossi spoke to them every day with devotional and spiritual lectures. Their first spiritual guide, Fr. Rocchi, traveled back to Nova Trento to give a series of talks to his beloved "nurses."

Amabile and the girls had been wearing the clothes of a typical peasant country girl—a long dress down to the ankles covered by an apron, and a *babushka* or kerchief around their heads. This had been the international dress of peasant women for centuries.

The girls had never seen a religious habit except in pictures of the saints. When Fr. Rossi asked them what kind of habit they wanted to wear, he showed them a picture of St. Margaret of Cortona which he had in his breviary as a bookmarker.

The girls wanted a black habit with a cincture of blue around the waist in honor of their patroness, Our Lady of the Immaculate Conception. Fr. Rossi asked if they could make habits like the one in the picture of St. Margaret. The girls replied eagerly that they could, for they had become expert seamstresses while making clothes for the poor.

The last step before the clothing ceremony was to choose a new religious name as was the custom for those entering a new way of life. To these young women the new garb and a new name meant a total dedication to Jesus Christ. They would witness to the whole world that they belonged only to the service of God and God's people.

Amabile chose the name of Sister Pauline of the Agonizing Heart Of Jesus. Virginia Nicolodi chose Sister Matilda of the Immaculate Conception and Theresa Maoli became Sister Inez of St. Joseph.

On December 7, 1895, Fr. Rossi invited the families of Amabile, Virginia and Theresa to the small chapel of the Little Hospital for the great day of investiture and their dedication as Sisters. Finally, the day of Amabile's dream, the day they had prayed and hoped for, arrived. After the sweat and tears of the past years, Our Mother's prophecy to Amabile had come to pass.

In the presence of their beloved families, these young pioneer women pronounced the vows of charity, obedience and chastity. The three Sisters were now dedicated to Jesus, Mary and Joseph. The new foundation of Sisters had chosen the name, the Little Sisters of the Immaculate Conception with the permission and blessing of the bishop.

There were tears of joy and happiness as the families embraced the new Sisters. The three families bonded with each other. They were greatly pleased that God had chosen their daughters for His very own.

Fr. Rossi wanted to introduce the new Sisters to the entire parish of Nova Trento and Vigolo. On December 8, 1895, the Feast of the Immaculate Conception, he invited all the parishioners to a liturgical celebration for the new Sisters. At ten o'clock in the morning a Solemn High Mass was celebrated with a grand procession of the Children of Mary and the various societies of the Church.

Caught up with great emotion, the people sang the hymns and songs of Italy and the Tyrol, joyfully and with gusto. The Children of Mary made crowns of flowers for the new Sisters. Before Mass Fr. Rossi put a crown upon the head of each Sister.

Fr. Rossi, in a voice laden with emotion, told everyone that this was a most extraordinary moment in the history of Nova Trento. In fact, it was a day of great significance not only for the state of Santa Catarina, but for all of Brazil. This was the first congregation of women religious founded in Brazil.

The three young girls, with their holy habits, their religious vows, and their determination to serve God, had begun a Brazilian congregation in the deep forests of a frontier land of the new world. Fr. Rossi's words would be prophetic.

The Sisters would plant the Gospel of Jesus Christ not only in Brazil, but in many nations. Three seemingly illiterate, unschooled young girls began hospitals, schools, orphanages and economic cooperatives, helping the poor, sick and abandoned. It all began in that little wooden shack in Vigolo.

The majority of the people were overwhelmed with happiness. "How marvelous are the ways of God!" They now had their own Little Sisters. Napoleone and the other families were being congratulated, and the Sisters' families were thanking God for His goodness.

Not everyone was happy, however. There were quite a few people, even some priests, who thought that these ignorant country girls would bring shame to Nova Trento. Some felt that the bishop had been deluded by the so-called humility of the girls, and that he had approved the new community because they could never qualify to become "true" religious Sisters.

In spite of the opposition, the new Sisters continued their great work of love for all. Many young women were fascinated with Sister Pauline's work, and the number of girls grew. Young girls from Nova Trento and Vigolo flocked to become Sisters.

Only two months later a new novitiate class of 11 girls had to be initiated. It was called the Novitiate of the Holy Purification.

Sister Pauline was happy, but the responsibility for these young women weighed upon her shoulders. What would she do with all these girls who wanted to become Sisters? Where would she house them? She needed more room and financial help to support the growing community.

The people of Vigolo begged Sister Pauline to send a few Sisters to Vigolo to care for their church, hospital, and the education of their children. She sent Sister Matilda (Virginia Nicolodi), and two novices, Theresa Valiate and Virginia Cestari.

Fr. Carlo Bonanni, the superior of the Jesuits in Brazil, made a canonical visit to Nova Trento in 1896. After seeing the growth of the religious community of Sisters, he told Fr. Rossi that this group was surely a miracle of God's grace.

The superior said to Fr. Rossi, "We must find more space for these young Sisters. You are the founding father and Sister Pauline is the founding mother. Both of you have the responsibility for the care of these souls. Visit this convent frequently, preach retreats each month, and have an eight-day retreat each year."

The economic problem for the community became more serious because Sister Pauline had begun an orphanage for boys and girls. The children needed clothes and food. Sister Pauline had to rent another building to house the children. The land which the Sisters culti-vated for harvest did not provide enough for the orphans, the sick, and the Sisters.

Sister Pauline prayed for guidance. One day at prayer she implored, "Oh God, You are so generous. My dreams, my hopes are now being fulfilled, but I can do nothing without You. I need to live in You, with You, through You, and with the help of my Immaculate Mother and St. Joseph, the family of dear Jesus, I must be able to maintain our good works."

During her prayers she was inspired by the Holy Spirit. She thought of a house near the convent, owned by Carlo Kramer, which she could use as a mill to make silk.

When she was a little girl in Vigolo Vattaro, Italy, she had worked in a silk mill. After some thought, she remembered what to do. She had to grow silk worms and get spinning machines to make cloth. Perhaps she could even make silk vestments for the church in Brazil! What an ambitious project! Was this a pipe dream? Or could Sister Pauline really accomplish this challenge?

In the city of Brusque, about forty miles from Nova Trento, lived Fr. Antonio Eising, a Franciscan priest. He was the pastor of the parish of Brusque and a very good friend of Fr. Rossi. Sister Pauline and a companion went to visit the priest at the suggestion of Fr. Rossi.

Fr. Eising was a kind and holy priest willing to help Sister Pauline in her search for the equipment necessary to start the silk mill. He introduced Sister Pauline to Mr. Charles Bauer who owned a factory in Brusque. This gentleman showed great kindness to Sister. He was instrumental in getting the mill started for the Sisters.

Mr. Carlo Kramer gave the Sisters a warehouse which was near their convent in Nova Trento. It was in this warehouse that Sister Pauline, after a novena to St. Joseph, began her new project. After getting the silk worms and raising the cocoons, they were ready to spin and dye the threads. From these threads was fashioned the finest silk in Brazil.

In addition to working in the fields and caring for the sick and orphans, all the Sisters, novices and postulants worked in the silk mill. Sister Pauline taught each one her job in the mill. This little country girl initiated a successful business deep in the forests of Brazil. The insignificant town of Nova Trento became a place famous for beautiful silk vestments.

The Sisters made exquisite silk fabrics which were sent all over the world. They received numerous awards from many nations and industrial expositions for the beauty and excellent workmanship of their silk.

With the money made from the mill, Mother Pauline asked her father, Napoleone, to construct a two story building to house all the orphans. Napoleone, who was still actively engaged in the construction business, built a solid building of stone and brick which is still standing and in use to this day.

The new orphanage was dedicated on the Feast of St. Agnes, 1897. There was plenty of room for the Sisters and orphans. Amabile's dreams were becoming a reality!

Life for the small community was never easy. The Sisters purchased a cow and started to raise chickens so the children would have milk and eggs. They worked hard on the land, in the mill, and in the various duties of church and school. Yet they continued to run out of the necessities.

One day, Fr. Rossi went to the convent to ask Mother Pauline how things were going. She said, "Father, we have run out of salt, and we have no money to buy any." To lighten the burden, Fr. Rossi said with his wry humor, "Let's baptize this house with the name Salamanca." The words *il sale manca* in Italian mean "the salt is missing."

The house is still called Salamanca. When I first heard the name, I presumed it was Spanish in origin, perhaps given by one of the Spanish priests. An older Sister explained to me that the origin of the name was a joke that stuck. It was, however, a serious expression of the poverty of those early days.

People from the area helped the Sisters and orphans. Costanza Valli, the wife of Giovanni Valli, was a great help to the Sisters as she organized the numerous works and charities.

Mother Pauline constantly went to St. Joseph with her economic problems, praying, lamenting, begging him to help in their daily needs. One day, Mother Pauline, after the last day of a novena to St. Joseph, cried out to him for help for her beloved orphans saying, "St. Joseph, you have never failed us!" A few hours after her prayer, a woman and her husband brought fifty chickens to the convent. Thus the chicken farm was begun, and an abundance of eggs were available for the children and Sisters.

After the two year novitiate was completed, Mother Pauline gave the following appointments: prefect of the boarding school for girls which Mother established in Nova Trento, nursing attendant, teacher of novices, and head of the silk mill. She soon found the value of each and every Sister in her young community. With her innate intelligence she realized that the growing community needed a personal rule of life and a constitution fashioned for their particular needs.

The new community wanted to write their own rule of life, but they would once again need guidance. Mother Pauline turned once more to Fr. Rossi's sister, Mother Angelica, the Abbess of Forli in Italy. She advised Mother Pauline and the Sisters to discover their chief mission among God's people. Then they could build their rule of life in the world around this mission.

Much prayer and thoughtful meditation was given to the new rule of life. They asked, "What are the limits?" "What can be accomplished for Christ within the boundaries of our talents and resources?" "How can we serve others and yet continue to attract vocations?" "How can we properly train the postulants and novices?" "Should we speak Portuguese in the community, since it is the language of Brazil?"

The strength of spirit and body which the Sisters exhibited was truly fantastic. Filled with the spirit of organization, Mother Pauline assigned to the Sisters their various responsibilities. They worked in the factory and fields, took care of the aged and orphans, and cared for the sick and handicapped in the home visitation program. They cleaned, cooked and sewed, made artificial flowers for sale, taught catechism, and cleaned the churches and sanctuaries. The work was never-ending. The energy came from Jesus Christ through the intercession of Our Blessed Mother and the leadership of Mother Pauline. She was their guide—their leader; she would show the way.

Mother Pauline frequently told the Sisters that their mission was not only in Vigolo and Nova Trento, but across the sea, on the mountains, in the deserts and forests of Brazil.

CHAPTER 11

Stability and Growth

Postulants and novices kept multiplying; in 1899 seven more novices were professed and eleven postulants accepted. Mother Pauline said to Fr. Rossi, "Nothing is easy, but everything is a miraculous occurrence."

With the help of Mother Angelica in Italy, Mother Pauline and her Sisters completed the Constitution of the Little Sisters of the Immaculate Conception. After Fr. Rossi read and approved it, the constitution was sent to the Bishop of Curitiba, Bishop Camargo Barros.

Bishop Barros, with the permission of Rome, happily approved the constitution and the Sisters entered the twentieth century as an authentic religious congregation of the Roman Catholic Church.

A young woman entered the novitiate in 1899. She was a brilliant and talented student named Sabina Bottamedi. During the beginning of her novitiate, Sabina began experiencing strange fantasies. She spoke unknown languages, screamed before religious statues, and predicted future events. Her behavior was a sign of demonic possession.

Mother Pauline and Fr. Rossi realized that the devil wanted to stop this woman from becoming a professed Sister. Sabina herself had no memory of the outbursts and prayed with the Sisters to do God's will.

Fr. Rossi decided to perform the rite of exorcism on Sabina. He urged her to take her religious vows immediately, even though she was eight months short of the two years needed to fulfill the novitiate.

At 7:00 a.m. on the Feast of St. Joseph, Sabina had a strong seizure. The Sisters started to pray with their arms outstretched, each one looking like a cross. Fr. Rossi composed the following prayer for the Sisters to say during the exorcism. "We beseech thee, O Lord, to liberate Sabina from this evil." They repeated this prayer for two hours, while Fr. Rossi read from the Scriptures and the rite of exorcism.

After two hours had passed, Sabina made her profession of faith and accepted her place as a professed Sister. The demon left her. She never again experienced the horror of another seizure. Everyone was convinced that the devil had not wanted her to become a religious Sister.

Fr. Rossi felt that the evil one was trying to ruin the work of the missions in Brazil, especially in Nova Trento, where there was such deep faith and love of God. He was so impressed and frightened with the demonic happenings surrounding Sister Sabina's novitiate, that he wrote to the Holy Father in Rome to obtain a special consecration for his flock. A few months later, Pope Leo XIII sent Fr. Rossi a blessing for strength and grace.

Sabina became Sister Vincenza Theodora of the Immaculate Conception. She became the teacher of novices. Her wisdom and keen intellect guided the sisters to become a Pontifical Institute. No wonder the devil did not want her to become a nun!

In 1900, many cities througout Brazil wanted to commemorate the beginning of the new century by placing statues of Christ the Redeemer on top of the mountains that guarded the cities. The greatest of these statues towered high above Rio de Janeiro.

The people of Nova Trento wanted to put a statue above their town. Many families imitated this practice by building large crosses on their homes and properties. The Sisters did likewise. Fr. Rossi and Mother Pauline dedicated a large, beautiful cross which the Sisters fashioned. They called it the Cross of the Congregation.

In each house of the congregation there is a reproduction of this cross. It is composed of the elements of the Passion, with the spear, the sponge, and a medallion of the Sacred Heart of Jesus superimposed upon the cross. In the center of the cross is a medallion of the Eucharist, with a chalice holding the Precious Blood and Body of Christ. At the base of the cross is the logo of the Congregation of the Little Sisters of the Immaculate Conception and a reliquary.

The candidates for Sisterhood and the Sisters were multiplying. The community needed a bell to signal the various activities. Since they were too poor to buy a proper bell, Mother found a piece of iron and hung it from a ceiling. When the iron was struck, it rang out admirably.

Their schedule was as follows: at 3:30 a.m. the first bell sounded for all in the community to get out of bed, pray, wash, etc., followed by a long period of meditation. Then they walked to the parish church where Holy Mass was celebrated by Fr. Rossi at 5:00 a.m.

For breakfast they usually had *polenta* with onion sauce. Afterward, each Sister, novice and postulant was assigned by Mother Pauline to work either at the orphanage, the school, the hospital infirmary, or the silk mill. Mother Pauline gloried in the work of the fields. She loved the earth, telling the Sisters, "If the earth is taken care of, it will be fruitful, because it is a gift to us from God." She always guided a small group of Sisters to the fields which her father, Napoleone, had given to the Sisters. They would work in silence interrupted only by prayer and hymns.

At noon, the Sisters returned from work to pray the fifteen decades of the rosary. After singing the Angelus, they sat down to a spartan lunch of leftover *polenta,* a hard boiled egg, or perhaps a piece of *luganica* (dry sausage).

Immediately after lunch, all the Sisters returned to work until 6:00 p.m. A frugal dinner of *minestra* (vegetable soup) and bread was shared by the Sisters. After dinner there was community prayer, followed by sewing, general repair of the orphans' clothing, and the making of artificial flowers for sale.

Some worked deep into the night. Others went to the chapel for private prayer and adoration. Mother Pauline had a great devotion to Jesus in the Most Blessed Sacrament. She encouraged the Sisters to realize that their strength and spiritual nourishment came from the Lord in the Blessed Sacrament.

The Mysteries of the Incarnation, the Passion, and the Death of Jesus Christ were the central themes of the meditations offered by Mother Pauline. The Blessed Mother was her mentor, for she had called her to the service of her Divine Son.

Mother Pauline's program was very simple: practice all the virtues, and love others. "To love, to care for others, and to pray must be the motto of our congregation. Be generous with Our Lord Jesus. Be generous with His people. We are to be always occupied in the things of Our Father. We must live for Him and obey His holy will in all matters."

Each month, Fr. Eising, pastor of the church in Brusque, would give the Sisters a day of recollection. He was a very holy priest, and the Sisters loved him.

In one of Fr. Eising's letters to Fr. Rossi, he said that he could truly feel the presence of the Holy Spirit in that little convent. The days spent with the Sisters were joyful and spiritually fulfilling for him.

There are a number of incidents which occurred in those first years that demonstrate the deep and simple faith of the Sisters. One day the Sister who cooked came to Mother Pauline and told her that there was nothing for the Sisters to eat. After the orphans had been fed and everyone was satisfied, there was no food remaining for the Sisters.

Mother Pauline said, "Let us say a prayer to St. Joseph. He will take care of us. He never fails to help."

They prayed and within an hour, a young girl from Nova Trento came with five dozen eggs for the Sisters. The girl said that she was going to take the eggs to market in order to sell them, but decided instead to take them to the convent. She did not know what had changed her mind.

There were many such stories of St. Joseph's aid in times of need and peril. Mrs. Giovanni Valli, a great benefactor of the Sisters, was frequently moved by the Spirit to take baskets of food to the Sisters. She said that she seemed to know when there was a need at the convent.

The orphans were always cared for first and the Sisters took what was left. The children were Mother Pauline's primary concern. Even though she had had a late start in her own schooling, Mother was determined to have a school for all the children of Nova Trento.

With her courage, persistence and determination, she eventually convinced the governmental authorities that a school was necessary for the children of Nova Trento and Vigolo.

CHAPTER 12

Growth and Crises

A group of 47 Polish immigrant families lived twenty miles from Nova Trento. They had moved to the town of Vignale from the interior of Santa Caterina, Brazil. The Polish families had immigrated to Brazil in 1878. Their farms were located on the border of the hostile Indian territory.

Five years after the Polish immigrants had established farms, the Indians began attacking them. The Indians continued to harass them and burn their farms for about six years. Many people were killed and the survivors began to move closer to the area of established authority.

These Polish immigrants were very devout and close to the Church, but they did not have their own priests. Instead, the Italian Jesuits worked among them. The older people had a difficult time understanding the sermons. Fortunately, many of the children spoke Italian and Portuguese and were able to translate what Father said.

In 1900, four young Polish girls entered Mother Pauline's Little Sisters. The first professed Sister was Maria Witkowski who took the name of Sister Mary Dorothea.

Today, in Brazil, there are many Sisters of Polish descent in the Congregation of the Little Sisters of the Immaculate Conception.

More and more young women came to Mother Pauline

seeking entrance to the congregation. The work of the congregation spread to the nearby town of Brusque and to the German community of Blumenthal. The Franciscans, who took care of many parishes in the area, sent many girls to Mother Pauline and the new congregation of Brazilian Sisters.

One day John and Maria Tonet brought their nineteen year old daughter, Catherine, to Mother Pauline. Catherine had hoped and dreamed for the day when she could become a Sister. She had been born in Brazil, but her parents had emigrated from the Lombardy region of Italy.

Mother saw in Catherine a beautiful soul, filled with love and God's grace. The only problem was Catherine's health. She had always been in poor health. In spite of this, Mother felt that Catherine's intelligence and deep spirituality would be an asset to the congregation.

Catherine was able to make her vows, taking the name of Sister Mary Bernadine. She remained for a time in the house at Nova Trento. Later, Mother sent her to the house in Vigolo. She felt the country air would benefit her.

One night, Mother Pauline dreamt she was in a field covered with beautiful flowers of various colors. In the midst of the flowers was the Virgin of Lourdes. Our Lady pointed to the flowers and the flowers suddenly evolved into young children dressed in white. The Lady said to Mother Pauline, "Look, my daughter, these are the children you will influence. They will be part of your life."

As Mother Pauline looked on, the Lady turned and pointed once more to the children and they became white flowers. The Lady bent down and picked a flower saying, "I will give this one to my beloved Son. It is the first pure flower of your children to go to glory. Be happy for Sister Bernadine."

A few days after the dream, Sister Bernadine died in sanctity and the Sisters, amid both tears and joy, gave this young Sister back to God. The first Sister born in Brazil became the first flower to be taken from the garden of the Virgin Mary. At the funeral of that sainted Sister, the people arrived in tremendous numbers. Everybody seemed to have known her. They had great respect for her and there were many expressions of emotion on the part of the people who believed, "An angel has gone home to Heaven."

Fr. Rossi was visiting Bishop Barros in Curitiba when Sister Bernadine died. The bishop received a telegram from Mother Pauline telling him of the Little Sister's death. He told Fr. Rossi about her death, and embracing the spiritual father, he said, "Father, this Sister is in Heaven."

Mother Pauline had many other prophetic dreams in her lifetime such as the knowledge of the earthquake that destroyed the city of Martescenio in Brazil.

To the very young, Mother Pauline would say, "Pray that you will soon be a candidate for the congregation. As you wait for the proper age to enter, study your lessons, pray your office, attend daily Mass, read the Scriptures, and learn the catechism."

Mother tried to instill in the postulants and novices a sense of appreciation for the written word, especially the Scriptures. She believed that Holy Scripture illumined the whole of their religious lives.

Work, prayer, mortification and study all helped to provide the proper setting for intimate conversation with Our Lord. Mother Pauline was ahead of her time as she begged the priests for lectures about Scripture. She realized sadly that she had had little training in the Word of God which she loved so much. She wanted her Sisters to have the opportunity to learn more and more about the life of faith.

There was more sadness for Mother Pauline and the Sisters when they learned that Fr. Rossi was being transferred to the great city of São Paulo. He was appointed the superior of the Jesuit Missions.

Fr. Rossi was a man of courage and wisdom. He had vision, zeal, humility and an iron will with a gentle temperament. As co-founder of the Little Sisters, he was the spiritual father of Mother Pauline and all the Little Sisters.

Now he was leaving them! How could they continue to exist? Would this be the end of the congregation? Mother Pauline prayed for strength. She tried to calm the fears of the Sisters and the people of the parish. "God will provide," she told them. "We have not come this far so that God will abandon us. Have faith."

The people of Nova Trento were desperately upset because they felt that the successful growth of Nova Trento was due to the stability and persevering work of Fr. Rossi. In the midst of the turmoil, Fr. Rossi tried to show them that this transfer was the will of God. He told them that the work of the Sisters and the growth of the town would never be discarded. Everything would continue with ever greater success in the name of Jesus.

Fr. Rossi assured everyone that there would be priests to continue the work of ministering to them. The Sisters would always have good spiritual directors and the counsel of the bishop.

On February 2, 1903, Mother Pauline, the Sisters and all the faithful gathered to say goodbye to Father. She felt the sadness of loss, but she had faith in the goodness of God. She knew instinctively that the congregation was the work of Jesus, Mary and Joseph, and destined to live on.

A week before Fr. Rossi moved away from his beloved Nova Trento, he assembled the Sisters to give them general directions. A formal, canonical election was held for the various administrative offices in the growing congregation. Mother Pauline was elected Mother General and the young Sister Theodora (Sabina Bottamedi) was made Vicar General.

Four months after Fr. Rossi's departure to São Paulo, Mother Pauline received a letter from Father that would change her whole life. Fr. Rossi asked Mother Pauline for a tremendous favor. He asked Mother and several Sisters to establish a house in São Paulo.

Fr. Rossi's letter instructed Mother to take with her to São Paulo Sister Louisa, Sister Serafina, and a young postulant by the name of Guiseppina Perreira who was fluent in Portuguese and was born of an Italian mother and Portuguese father.

The letter also instructed Mother to ask a trustworthy Christian man to accompany them to São Paulo. Sister Vincent was to take Mother's place in Nova Trento as director of the Little Sisters.

Father wrote, "Do not be afraid. This is God's will. There is so much to be done here! Your dreams will become a reality! God will allow your sacrifices and prayers to bear fruit in this new mission. There will be many vocations in São Paulo. The ex-slaves and their children need your help. God is showing us a great challenge. Please come!"

When Napoleone heard about the request, he was extremely upset. Knowing his daughter's determination, he said, "I am going to accompany you and the other Sisters. I will not allow you to go with anyone else."

Napoleone, the good papa, wanted to see what was in store for his beloved daughter. From the money he had saved, he was able to pay the passage for the group.

The spirits of the Sisters soared. They were being asked to be missionaries, Christ's ambassadors to the big city! With tears of joy mixed with sadness and thanksgiving, they were about to enter upon a fantastic adventure—the work of the Church for the cause of Christ!

The Sisters prostrated themselves before Jesus in the Blessed Sacrament, asking the Lord to take them to the city to help the sick, the dying, the abandoned, and all who needed care. Mother Pauline understood that God had plans for the congregation outside of Santa Catarina. She had to leave the land she had lived in and known since she was eight years old.

The small group departed from Nova Trento amidst tears and kisses. They left by horse and wagon on July 17, 1903, and arrived at the Port of Itajai. On the same day they left by ship for the city of Santos.

Napoleone had many doubts. He could not understand why his little girl wanted to go to the big city. He was afraid for her. He would not be nearby to protect her. Napoleone had a sense of foreboding. He would have to leave them there alone. He prayed for trust in God and committed them to the care of Jesus and Mary.

After a long and tedious voyage, the four Sisters were met by Fr. Gaetano Benvenuti, a fellow Jesuit of Fr. Rossi, who took them to São Paulo at Fr. Rossi's request. When Fr. Gaetano met the Sisters he thought, "Fr. Rossi must be crazy having these country girls come to this city of São Paulo. They don't even know how to speak Portuguese!"

With the exception of Giussepina, the postulant, who knew Portuguese, the Sisters spoke only Italian. Father Gaetano wondered how they would work among people who spoke only Portuguese. He was instructed by Fr. Rossi to take the group to a convent compound called the House of the Good Shepherd where he would meet with them.

It was at this convent that Mother Pauline and her Little Sisters met other religious Sisters for the first time in their lives. After Napoleone had reluctantly returned home, Mother Pauline and the Sisters lived with the religious of the Good Shepherd for five months. Here they learned some Portuguese and became acquainted with many of the customs of the people in the São Paulo area.

Mother Pauline had a difficult time learning the Portuguese language. For the rest of her life, she wrote and spoke a mixture of Italian and broken Portuguese.

CHAPTER 13

The Challenge Accepted

Fr. Rossi told Mother and the Sisters they would live in the hill section of Ipiranga, a suburb of São Paulo. There was an abandoned church and house in the area. The very first benefactor of the Little Sisters in São Paulo was Count José De Azevedo. He bought the land and renovated the church and the house directly behind the church. The church and house were joined by a hall and meeting room.

Mother Pauline was very grateful to Count De Azevedo for his generosity and said to him, "My thanks mean nothing, but I shall let the Lord thank you for me. I cannot repay you. May the Lord repay your kindness."

After five months with the Sisters of the Good Shepherd, the small group had to leave the comfort and joy of their warm and loving new friends. The Mother Superior of the Good Shepherd Convent told them, "This convent shall always be your home. You are a blessing to us and have come with much needed help for the people of God."

The Vicar General of the diocese came and celebrated Mass in the church which the Sisters named the Chapel of the Holy Family. In his sermon, the priest told the Sisters that their work was to be among the ex-slaves. "Your work will be most precious in the eyes of God because it must make up for the years of maltreatment and injustice towards the slaves."

On the vigil of the Feast of the Immaculate Conception in 1903, the Sisters moved into their primitive home.

Bishop Barros de Camargo of the Diocese of Curitiba was transferred to the See of the Diocese of São Paulo. The Sisters were blessed when he came to them. Through the kindness of Bishop Barros, many benefactors came to visit the Sisters' new foundation. One of the most outstanding friends among the benefactors was Mrs. Anna Brotero DeBaros. Senhora Anna DeBaros was the recent widow of a wealthy industrialist. The devout couple had been childless, but they were most generous to the orphaned children of São Paulo.

Mother Pauline was anxious to set up an orphanage for the poor children of the ex-slaves. Many had come from the northern part of Brazil after gaining their independence.

With the tremendous aid of Senhora Anna, Mother built an orphanage on the property close to the chapel.

Senhora Anna gave vast amounts of money to the maintenance of the orphans. She encouraged others in her society to give with Christian charity to this great cause. Anna was later elected to the presidency of the Institute of the Holy Family, an organization founded for the benefit of the orphans in the Holy Family Orphanage.

The Congregation of the Little Sisters was finding it financially difficult to maintain its good works in Nova Trento and São Paulo. There was so much poverty in Brazil that supporting the orphans and the aged, and operating adequate hospitals created an economic burden upon the young community.

Mother Vincent Bottamedi in Nova Trento struggled with the debt that had been left by Fr. Rossi and Mother Pauline. There was much animosity toward Mother Pauline because she had left Nova Trento for São Paulo. The creditors felt that they would lose everything because they thought that Mother Pauline had absconded with the money and that Fr. Rossi had defrauded them. Why else had Mother Pauline gone to São Paulo, and why else the secrecy of her departure? The creditors took the one cow the Sisters had for the orphanage. They removed the chickens from the property and confiscated anything that could be carried away.

The priests did not know how to help and many people turned against them. Fr. Rossi and Mother Pauline were called hypocrites. Some benefactors stopped their donations to the good works of the community.

Mother Vincent, with God's help, knew her first task was to make sure the life of the religious community was not disturbed. She did not want the novices and postulants to become depressed and anxious, nor did she want the girls who were interested in joining them to lose their holy vocation. Mother Vincent continued to visit the creditors in order to calm them and assure them of payment. They humiliated her, but with wisdom, humility, and patience she bowed before her accusers and begged them to understand.

The smile and good humor of Mother Vincent Bottamedi gave comfort to the Sisters and she surmounted the pain with unfailing love for all. Eventually, through her God-given talents as an administrator, all was paid. She was at this time in her life only 24 years of age.

In one of Mother Vincent's letters to Mother Pauline, she wrote, "God is putting us to the test. Your absence has left us like a ship without a sail, with only two stars to guide us, Jesus and Mary. My blood runs cold every time I must make a decision, but I have faith in God. I seek courage from the Virgin Mary. I know the Lord Jesus is with me. Mary and St. Joseph are guiding us. I know you are praying for us. Blessed be God! I love you, dear Mother. I pray for your work in São Paulo. Continue to remember us. We are so far away from you."

The Sisters in Nova Trento worked harder and reduced their spending. Seeing their enthusiasm, the children

pitched in and helped as much as possible on the land
work and the work of the orphanage.

When the troubles were over and the financial difficulty
had passed, they wrote Mother Pauline telling her not to
worry. They exulted, "Things are getting better!"

The successor to Bishop Barros in Curitiba was Bishop
Leopold Duarte. He came to Nova Trento for a pastoral
visit from the 12th to the 19th of August, 1905. He was
immensely impressed with the work of the Little Sisters.
He was particularly moved by the evangelical spirit of the
small community.

When Mother Vincent met Bishop Duarte for the first
time, she wrote in her journal that a voice within her said,
"This is my servant who will help your congregation."

Bishop Duarte saw that the community of Sisters was
struggling financially. He asked an influential and wealthy
citizen of Nova Trento to dedicate himself to the Sisters.
The man whom the bishop chose was Francesco Gotardi,
a devout Christian who totally gave himself to the financial needs of the community's good works.

Meanwhile, in São Paulo, Mother Pauline was asked by
Bishop Barros to send Sisters to a hospital and an old
age home in Braganza. The hospital was located 65 miles
away from São Paulo and was in need of direction and
personnel.

Mother Pauline asked Mother Vincent to send several
Sisters from Nova Trento who would be able to do the
work required. Mother Vincent sent three Sisters who,
together with Mother Pauline and Sister Serafina,
established a house in Braganza.

After Mother Pauline directed the initial work of
Braganza, she returned to São Paulo. Sister Francesca was
nominated superior of the Hospital of St. Vincent de Paul
in Braganza.

The work of the Little Sisters was growing by leaps and
bounds. The bishop asked for more Sisters to open a
hospital for men, and also a center for the terminally ill.

Mother Pauline asked Mother Vincent for more Sisters to be sent to São Paulo. Four more Sisters were sent from Nova Trento in 1904.

During this period, many young women from São Paulo and Braganza asked to enter the community of the Little Sisters of the Immaculate Conception. The young girls from the São Paulo area made their postulancy at the House of the Holy Family in São Paulo and took their novitiate in Nova Trento.

In the Roman Catholic Church, each bishop in the world must visit the Vatican in Rome in order to make a report on the condition and care of the diocese entrusted to him. This is called the *"ad limina* visit" and is made every five years. In 1905 Bishop Barros made his visit to Rome. Sadly, upon the bishop's return trip, his ship was sunk off the coast of Spain. This caused massive grief in his diocese and especially among Mother Pauline and the Little Sisters.

The growth of the congregation in São Paulo was due in great part to the help and confidence of Bishop Barros. Six months after his death, Mother Pauline's grief was lightened by the appointment of Bishop Leopold Duarte, taking the place of Bishop Barros for the second time, as the first Archbishop of São Paulo.

Archbishop Duarte knew the Sisters from his former Diocese of Curitiba. He admired their enthusiastic work and spirit of Christian charity. The new archbishop wanted the Sisters to take over the Maritime Home for Retired Sailors who had no families. This home plus two hospitals were given to the Sisters' care.

The stupendous growth of Mother Pauline's work in the area outside of Nova Trento strained the resources of the community. Mother Pauline had no head for figures. She was an untiring worker, but was childlike in her approach to the many administrative tasks of her growing congregation. She frequently said, "God will provide. Let us love Jesus and nothing more." When she came to São Paulo she had nothing—she depended on prayer. "This is God's work. He will show us the way."

Sister Serafina, Mother Pauline's secretary and assistant, was given much of the administrative work of the congregation in São Paulo. She was a brilliant and gifted woman with great personal charm. Her wit and intelligence gave her the ability to communicate with everyone. Today we would call her a genius in public relations.

Mother Pauline had total confidence in Sister Serafina and gave her much authority and responsibility. Unfortunately, Sister Serafina was overly ambitious and self-seeking.

Sister Serafina enjoyed the company of the wealthy benefactors and entered their society with ease. She became particularly friendly with the wealthy widow, Anna Brotero DeBaros. Anna was completely charmed by Sister Serafina and she spent many hours each day with Sister.

It was not unusual that Senhora Anna spent time with the administrator since she was president of the Society of the Holy Family. But Senhora Anna also spent many nights in the convent. In those days it was almost unheard of for a lay person to stay the night in the convent so often.

Many Sisters in the community felt that Sister Serafina was lax in adapting rules. They thought her to be worldly, selfish and divisive.

Even though Senhora Anna was most generous in giving to the congregation, there was a sense that Sister Serafina was exploiting this good woman. The Sisters saw that this relationship was developing into an unhealthy emotional bond.

Sister Serafina made no secret of telling everyone, including Mother Pauline, that the constitution of the congregation had to be reformed. She said the congregation was old-fashioned and its constitution was based excessively on a monastic rule.

At one time, Sister Serafina told Mother Pauline that Fr. Rossi was not interested in the Little Sisters anymore, and that he was going to form another group. She tried to sow dissension among the Sisters in São Paulo.

When several Sisters went to Mother Pauline to complain about Sister Serafina, Mother defended her and told them of her work for the congregation. Mother told the Sisters to be charitable in all things. "For those who love, much is forgiven," she would remind them.

CHAPTER 14

The Way of The Cross

Mother Pauline's and Fr. Rossi's responses to the complaints about Sister Serafina did not satisfy many of the Sisters. Neither the foundress nor the co-founder seemed troubled by the difficulties the Sisters were having with Sister Serafina. For the well being of their beloved congregation, the Sisters went to see Archbishop Duarte as a last resort. They made a very good case of their grievance against Sister Serafina. They had a list of signatures from the majority of the Sisters in São Paulo. But they were careful to exonerate Fr. Rossi and Mother Pauline, telling the archbishop that the two did not see Sister Serafina's duplicity.

Mother was so busy establishing new houses for the work of the Sisters, and Fr. Rossi was out of town so often, that it was extremely difficult for them to see the problem. To the community, Sister Serafina seemed to be undermining authority while hypocritically paying lip service to Mother Pauline.

Archbishop Duarte was very upset with the report. He reacted most severely. The first thing he did was to speak with Senhora Anna Brotero telling her of the impropriety of Sister's behavior. He asked her to stop seeing or speaking to Sister Serafina.

Senhora Anna realized that she was in the midst of a messy situation. She affirmed her desire to help the orphans and to continue her charitable work among the children. She told the archbishop, "I have no children of my own. All that I have, I give to Jesus through the Little Sisters of the Immaculate Conception."

Because Anna was a good and generous woman, the archbishop felt she had been victimized by Sister Serafina's ambitions. He asked her to continue her wonderful work for the community, but not through Sister Serafina.

After speaking with Senhora Anna, Archbishop Duarte called Fr. Rossi immediately. He gave Father these orders:

1. Sister Serafina was to be moved away from São Paulo and she was to be stripped of all authority. She was not to hold a position of authority in the Little Sisters again.
2. Mother Pauline was to be removed from the position of Mother General. She was never to hold any office in the congregation she founded. She was to spend the rest of her life as a simple Sister.
3. An election was to be held for the position of Mother General and other offices. Only the sisters from São Paulo were to vote. Those in Nova Trento were not to be told in order to allay the fears of the novices and not disturb the vocation process. Mother Pauline was not to be allowed as a candidate.
4. Mother Pauline was to return to Nova Trento and was to be given no financial responsibility.
5. Mother Pauline was to be called the Mother Foundress, but she was no longer to have a position of authority in the congregation of the Little Sisters of the Immaculate Conception.
6. A general chapter meeting was to be held as soon as possible after the election of a new Mother General. A revised or new constitution was to be planned and discussed.

Fr. Rossi was overcome with sadness and heartbreak as the archbishop told him what must be done. What a terrible cross for Mother Pauline! How could he tell her this awful news?

The archbishop was adamant. There was to be no change. Everything he had written had to be done for the good of souls and the congregation. Fr. Rossi was to tell all this to Mother Pauline.

Father was in tears. He worried about the effect of this horrible event upon Mother Pauline. It seemed so unfair to burden this saintly woman with yet another cross. He prostrated himself before the Blessed Sacrament and prayed for long hours. He begged the Lord for guidance—for some solution, some answer.

The decision of the archbishop sounded harsh to Fr. Rossi. He thought it would all pass over soon. Why upset Mother Pauline? He would tell her nothing, except to take a trip to Nova Trento. He would tell her that the Sisters needed her there to intensify the spiritual life of the novices. Her daughters in Nova Trento missed her and would be encouraged by her energy and example.

When Fr. Rossi asked Mother to go to Nova Trento, she was surprised that he seemed so insistent. She had always felt that Mother Vincent Theodora was doing a great job as the Mother Vicar and superior of Nova Trento. The novices who had been professed glowingly praised Mother Vincent.

Why should she return? There was so much work to be done in the building of new missions! Yet Fr. Rossi said she was needed in Nova Trento.

Out of obedience, Mother returned to Nova Trento. Her Sisters greeted her with unbounded joy. The people were delighted to have little Amabile back home in the country!

The Sisters who had been left in São Paulo felt weak and alone without Mother's presence. Fr. Rossi wrote to Mother Vincent telling her of the situation and the archbishop's demands. Mother Vincent was crushed. Why hadn't Mother Pauline been told of this? How could she continue to hide this from her?

Mother Pauline stayed one month in Nova Trento, and after seeing how well everything was functioning, she wanted to return to São Paulo. It was at this time that Mother Vincent told her of the difficulties in São Paulo. Fr. Rossi, in a letter to Mother Vincent, suggested that both Mother Pauline and Mother Vincent come to São Paulo and speak to the archbishop.

On August 13, 1909, both Mother Pauline and Mother Vincent went to visit the archbishop. The archbishop interpreted Mother Pauline's visit as a defiance of his orders and severely chastised her. He reiterated his demands and forbade her presence in São Paulo or Nova Trento. He told Mother Pauline she must go to Braganza in the Asylum of St. Vincent DePaul and work there as a simple Sister.

During the humiliation and chastisement, Mother Pauline kept her head bowed. She remained silent during the archbishop's litany of complaints against her. At the conclusion of the meeting, Mother Vincent tells us that Mother Pauline raised her head and said, "Your will shall be done, Your Excellency. I ask only that the Congregation of the Immaculate Conception remain intact. I pray that my weaknesses will in no way disturb the congregation. Whatever Your Excellency decides, I will adhere to. Your word is my command!"

Mother Vincent Bottamedi tried to explain to the archbishop that none of this was Mother Pauline's fault. Since Mother would not defend herself, Mother Vincent urged Archbishop Duarte to see Mother Pauline's innocence.

But the archbishop had made up his mind. Mother Vincent's explanation was to no avail. A judgment had been made and it would stand. On that day, the Way of the Cross began for Mother Pauline. This was an important turning point in Mother's life, the beginning of the hidden life of Blessed Pauline.

One may find it difficult to understand how this woman was able to tolerate the unjust humilation; how she who had labored so long and so fervently for Christ and His Church did not rebel against the injustice and false accusation.

It is in this event of Mother Pauline's life that we come to the crux of her spiritual identity. Her response to this trial with humility, obedience, and charity revealed the depth of her holiness.

The words of Holy Scripture burned in her heart as she listened to Archbishop Duarte's voice. *"Into your hands, O Lord, I commend my spirit,"* Jesus had prayed upon the cross. In the garden of Gethsemane, He had cried, *"Not my will, but Thine be done."*

There is a proverb that says, "God writes straight with crooked lines." God, our Father, tells us, *"My ways are not your ways."*

The words of Scriptural obedience entered Mother's mind. "This cross is the will of God. I must take up my cross and follow Christ."

The words of Our Blessed Mother echoed in her mind, *"Be it done unto me according to Thy word."*

Blessed Pauline was 44 years old when she was removed from her duties as Mother General. It would be another 33 years before the Lord Jesus would call her home to heaven.

Following the archbishop's orders, an election was held for the offices of Mother General and Mother Vicar. The new Mother General elected was Mother Vincent Theodora (Sabina Bottamedi). Mother Matilda (Virginia Nicolodi) was elected Vicar General. Fr. Rossi was named co-founder of the Little Sisters by Archbishop Duarte. Father continued as spiritual director. Mother Pauline was given the title of Mother Foundress.

Sister Serafina was transferred to the House of Mercy in San Carlos. She was the first professed Sister of the Congregation of the Little Sisters of the Immaculate

Conception to leave.

Many years later, Mother said, "I pray constantly for Serafina, because through my weakness and imprudence, I allowed her to fall into the trap of ambition and pride."

In 1909 the Little Sisters numbered 150 in 6 houses. In a letter to all the Sisters, Mother Pauline said she wanted to resign from the position of Mother General. The reason she gave was that she felt incompetent to continue leading the Sisters in a period of growth.

Mother Pauline also wrote that she wanted to follow the orders of the archbishop in perfect obedience by relinquishing all authority and becoming a simple subject of the community. She wanted to live and die as nothing more than a Little Sister.

The first Mother General elected during the general chapter meeting was Mother Vincent. When Mother Pauline knelt before her to kiss her hand and pledge her obedience, Mother Vincent, with tears in her eyes, lifted her up to kiss her. Mother Vincent and the Sisters knew what a terrible loss it would be for the congregation to see her go into exile.

A month later, Mother Pauline left São Paulo for Braganza to begin her work. Without bitterness or lament, this saintly heroine departed, smiling and hopeful that God had given her another opportunity to serve. The prophets of gloom, calling her dumb and naive, predicted she would leave the congregation because of this humiliation.

The hospital-asylum of St. Vincent de Paul in Braganza was the most humble house of the congregation. The poor patients in that institution were the sick, the abandoned, the handicapped, and the emotionally retarded. It was in this milieu that Mother Pauline would work and live for the next ten years of her life.

The Sisters at Braganza became utterly fascinated with their Mother Foundress. She chose the most humble, menial labor. She was the first to arrive at the chapel in the morning, and the last to leave at night. She spoke very little and carried herself with good cheer and courage.

Many people were surprised at Mother Pauline's humble acceptance of her degraded position. They were surprised because they did not know her holiness. She left São Paulo and went to Braganza simply because God willed it for her.

Carrying her little sack with the few personal belongings she owned, she renewed her commitment to Christ. She often said, "I came into this world with nothing and I shall leave it with nothing."

For little Amabile Visintainer, humiliation and deprivation were the ingredients of sanctity. To the world, her crisis was a disgrace. To her, it was the plan of God, so she used pain to become a saint.

CHAPTER 15

Victory In Suffering

In the asylum at Braganza, Mother Pauline chopped wood, scrubbed floors, and toiled in the vegetable garden. She cared for those among the handicapped and the aged who were sick and infirm. The Sisters reported that she inevitably chose the most difficult cases with whom to work.

It was at this time that she injured her finger while chopping wood. Upon examination, the doctor discovered she had chronic diabetes. The sores and cuts never healed. In spite of this she continued to work tirelessly.

During her ten years at Braganza, Mother Pauline wrote many letters of encouragement to other Sisters which contained no trace of regret. She also wrote many letters to Fr. Rossi. In one letter, she said, "I am in good health and I enjoy much peace. There is joy in poverty if it is offered to Jesus with love. I am content and happy in the Lord. Please do not worry about me."

The 20th anniversary of the founding of the congregation of the Little Sisters of the Immaculate Conception took place on July 12, 1910. Fr. Rossi celebrated the anniversary Mass in Braganza in the presence of Sister Isabelle, the superior, Mother Pauline, and Sister Stanislaus.

Mother Pauline, in a letter to the Sisters of the congregation, wrote, "It is with the most sublime joy that I tell you that our congregation is growing and doing the work of Jesus Christ among His people. Our spirit of religious poverty must always be an imitation of Jesus Christ."

Fr. Rossi in his many letters to Mother Pauline never mentioned anything about the crisis or her confinement to Braganza. One can only guess about the great sorrow he must have carried in his heart concerning the disastrous turn of events. We can read between the lines in his letters about the burden he carried.

Mother Pauline's dear father, Napoleone, died on March 6, 1911, at the age of 71. Now a great sorrow was added to her other suffering.

She wrote to Mother Vincent, the Superior General, "I am well, but sad at the death of my dearest father. I request, in your charity, dear Mother General, to tell the Sisters that I would be very grateful if they would continue to remember him in prayer."

Fr. Rossi also wrote to the Mother General saying, "He was my sincere friend. He accompanied me on many missions for the glory of God. Napoleone was my helpmate, my pillar and strength during my years in Nova Trento. Joy and peace to the just! He has surely gone now to the Kingdom of God where he is praying for us. The number of our intercessors is growing in heaven."

Napoleone Visintainer was a true hero of the Little Sisters because without his patience and understanding, there would never have been a Mother Pauline. To this day, he is remembered in the prayers of the congregation.

Mother Pauline grew in holiness and love by living a life of hard work and prayer. In her many letters to her family and the Sisters, she constantly wrote how happy she was that she did not have the cross of the whole congregation upon her shoulders and how good and loving our Father in heaven was to relieve her of the burden and give her such peace and joy.

The Sisters who worked with Mother Pauline at St. Vincent de Paul Asylum were encouraged by her energy, perseverance, and spirit of prayerfulness. She inspired them to greater heights of charity for the honor and glory of God. It was during this time that she was transformed into the great Mother Pauline of the Agonizing Heart of Jesus.

A second general chapter meeting was held in 1919. By now everyone had come to the conclusion that Mother Pauline was needed at the motherhouse which she had begun and a unanimous vote was taken to call her back to São Paulo. The novitiate was moved there from Nova Trento and a new building was constructed next to the motherhouse for the novices.

Mother Pauline was the light the congregation needed. Her intensity, love, and prayerful concern influenced generations of Sisters who passed through the motherhouse where she remained for the rest of her life.

Fr. Rossi was joyful beyond words when Mother Pauline returned to where he felt she had always belonged. He asked the archbishop and his Jesuit superiors if he could reside at the motherhouse. There was a small two-room building called the "hermitage" at the far end of the property. Fr. Rossi lived there until his death in 1921.

Archbishop Duarte, in one of his many visits to the motherhouse, passed the kitchen of the community and saw Mother Pauline cooking at the wood-burning stove, lifting a heavy pot. He said to the Sisters afterwards, "To find the foundress of a great religious congregation with a pot in her hand near a hot stove surely bodes well for that congregation."

Mother Pauline became the first general counselor and advisor to the Mother General. She made canonical visits with the Mother General to all the foundations of the Little Sisters. Each new foundation asked for Mother Pauline to come and stay with them a while. It was a real delight for the Sisters to have Mother with them, and to Mother it was Vigolo all over again.

Sadness entered Mother Pauline's life once more when her dear friend, the sweet and gentle Mother Matilda (Virginia Nicolodi), the friend of her youth, died on July 22, 1917. Amabile and Virginia had struggled together. Virginia had been Mother Pauline's most intimate friend. The friendship of these two most unusual women had endured for 41 years. It had all started in Vigolo when Amabile and Virginia, as young girls, had begun to work with the poor and suffering for the glory of Jesus, Mary and Joseph. Mother Matilda had become the vicar of the congregation, which meant she had been second in command to the Mother General. She had also been the historian of the congregation till her death. Virginia had always been ill, but she had accomplished a prodigious amount of work in the congregation.

More sorrow entered Mother Pauline's life when Fr. Rossi became very ill in the hermitage. On August 13, 1921, Fr. Rossi was brought into the motherhouse so that the Sisters could care for him. Mother Pauline personally took care of him with the Sister-Nurses to assist her.

While in the motherhouse, he dictated his spiritual last will and testament. This beautiful testament was a witness to the call he had received from God and to the privilege God had given him to have a part in the founding of the Little Sisters. He proclaimed the crucial role of Mother Pauline in founding the congregation and praised her humility and love.

On his deathbed, he said, "I leave now to go to the place that God has prepared for me. I trust that He will be gentle in His judgment. How sweet is this death, for it is taking me home to the Lord Jesus! I go to live in community with Jesus, Mary and Joseph. I leave my dear Sisters behind. Please remember me as your dear Father in Christ."

Present at his deathbed were Mother Pauline, Mother Vincent and three Sisters who had cared for him during his illness. He died peacefully in the arms of God on October 30, 1921.

Mother Pauline continued to work in the kitchen, the garden, and the infirmary. She chopped wood, cultivated mulberry trees for the silk worms she raised, and opened a silk mill on the grounds of the motherhouse just as she had in Nova Trento. This was the only way she knew to help support the ministries of the congregation.

Among the other crops, Mother Pauline raised sunflowers. The Sisters used the seeds for oil and fed the cattle with the stalks. A visitor to Brazil today will be greeted by huge fields of smiling sunflowers, with their petals open and their faces turned joyfully toward heaven.

Throughout Brazil the need for Sisters was tremendous. Bishops wrote for more Sisters to staff their parishes. They especially wanted the first Brazilian congregation, their very own, to come to all parts of Brazil.

Mother Pauline's fame as a charitable and loving person had spread throughout Brazil. People marveled at the life of holiness of this nun. They knew she was a child of immigrants, who came from the forests of Santa Catarina. Every week many people would make the trip to the hill of Ipiranga in São Paulo just to see Mother Pauline, kiss her hand, and ask her to pray for them. With a joyful countenance and love in her heart, she always had time for everyone. She loved all people.

CHAPTER 16

The Final Years of Pilgrimage

Mother Vincent Bottamedi had become increasingly ill during her 22 years as Mother General. She was elected unanimously to this position three times. She was recognized by all as an extraordinary woman.

We recall that she was the young novice troubled by evil spirits. The devil had tried to prevent this saintly woman from becoming a religious because he knew what God could accomplish through her. She was the instrument chosen by God for the spiritual and physical growth of the congregation of the Little Sisters.

Mother Vincent was a religious of great intelligence, energy, prudence, and wisdom. She possessed a prayerful spirit, a strong will, and a practical common sense.

As Superior General, she normalized and perfected the life of the congregation after the terrible crisis with Sister Serafina and the removal of Mother Pauline. She had never sought the position of Superior General, but when it was thrust upon her, she always kept in her heart a tremendous devotion and respect for Mother Foundress.

Mother Vincent had remained the dear friend of Mother Pauline. She had been among Blessed Pauline's first novices in Nova Trento and said frequently that she owed her religious life to Mother Pauline's example and love.

When Mother Vincent died on September 28, 1931, Mother Pauline cried in pain, saying the congregation owed so much to this immensely talented and holy Sister. At the time of her death, the congregation had 400 Sisters. They also had 40 new foundations, among them hospitals, orphanages, homes for the aged, and a college.

Archbishop Duarte held Mother Vincent in high esteem and celebrated her funeral Mass in the presence of many bishops, priests and religious. He wrote to Rome for a Decree of Praise for Mother Vincent which was received by the congregation. Six months later, Mother Vincent's younger sister, Sister Louise Bottamedi, was unanimously elected Mother General. Mother Pauline continued as First Counselor and accompanied Mother Louise on all canonical visits.

In 1938, Mother Pauline's chronic diabetes began affecting her eyes, causing increased loss of vision. The injury to her finger, which she had incurred while chopping wood many years before, never healed. A scab would form, and then break off and bleed, again and again.

Dr. José Vellela, the physician at the Sister's hospital, told Mother Pauline that gangrene had set in in the middle finger of her right hand. The finger had to be amputated to keep the infection from spreading.

Unfortunately, there were three amputations. The surgical amputation of her finger did not contain the spread of gangrene. A second operation was done to remove her right hand, and finally, Mother Pauline's right arm had to be amputated.

Sister Elmatrusa, a nurse at Mother Pauline's surgical amputation, said, "Mother Pauline had a sense of resignation and of joy."

She quoted Mother Pauline, who said, "I am unhappy that I will not be able to work as before, but my arm is not mine. It was given to me by God—His will be done. He wanted my finger, and then my hand; now He wants my arm. I give my whole being to Him! Behold, I give Him whatever He asks."

After her convalescence in the congregation's nursing

home in Braganza, Mother Pauline returned to the motherhouse in São Paulo. Each day Mother would continue to work in a small room which was set aside for the making of artificial flowers. The flowers were sold by the congregation to augment the meager income of the community.

The Sisters said Mother became very proficient in making the flowers with one arm. She would place the stem in her mouth and use her left hand to string the leaves, petals and blossoms. Mother had totally lost her eyesight, but she said, "Even if I cannot see, I can still work."

Each day Mother Pauline spent hours in prayer before the Most Blessed Sacrament. She prayed many rosaries, continually fingering the rosary beads at her side throughout the day. One could find her either in her workroom or in her special place in the chapel, the right side by the image of Our Lady of Lourdes.

The Little Sisters of the Immaculate Conception celebrated the 50th anniversary of their founding in 1940 in the presence of their Mother Foundress. They received the Decree of Praise from the Holy Father and became a Pontifical congregation of Sisters.

On the occasion of the 50th anniversary, Mother Pauline wanted a very simple celebration. She said they were a community of the poor for the poor. A High Mass was celebrated by their director, Fr. Angelo Gianella, who had been appointed by the Jesuit superior after the death of Fr. Rossi.

The Sisters received telegrams of congratulations from Rome and from many bishops, priests, and government officials in Brazil. Thousands of grateful Brazilians expressed their thanksgiving and praise for the work of the Little Sisters.

Mother Pauline was in her 75th year. She decided to leave a spiritual will to her beloved Sisters of the congregation. The short document from the archives of the Little Sisters of the Immaculate Conception is as follows:

My dearest children:

In this year of 1940, we rejoice that it has been 50 years since I left my father's house. I was called by God through His Most Holy Mother, Our Lady of Lourdes, and I responded with God's abiding grace. God did the rest. I did very little. I exhort you and recommend you to be humble, to have confidence in God, and to trust in Our Immaculate Mother. Be faithful spouses of Christ. Go forward with confidence, and hope in His love and mercy. Holy charity must always be your supreme virtue, especially love and care for the sick and aged.

Care for the children. Educate them in our holy Christian faith because they are the future of our Catholic Church. Love everybody and practice charity daily within your mind, heart and spirit.

My mission has ended and I shall die content in the knowledge that I have given what poor talents I have to my Lord and my All. I have made many mistakes, but I ask His mercy, for sometimes the "zeal of His house eateth us up."

I ask that you remember me in prayer so that God will be merciful in judging me. God bless each one of you. Love Jesus and only Him! Do charity and God will give the rest.

Mother Pauline became weaker shortly after the golden jubilee of the congregation. Mother Louise, the Mother General, firmly convinced her to remain in bed for part of the day. Blessed Pauline was finding it more difficult to walk and the Sisters feared she would fall.

On March 2, 1941, the doctor confined Mother Pauline to her bed since she had become very weak and was not able to stand without aid. Fifteen days later she received the Last Rites and Holy Viaticum given her by the new chaplain, Fr. Guido Deltoro.

Archbishop Duarte had died and his successor was
Archbishop Alfonesca DeSilva, who held Mother Pauline
in high esteem. Archbishop DeSilva came to Mother's
sickbed to bless and comfort her. He recommended her
to the whole archdiocese in prayer.

After two months of grave illness there seemed to be
remission in her suffering. The Sisters were joyful that
perhaps Mother had passed the crisis and would rally. But
about that time the doctors found that Mother Pauline
was suffering from pulmonary cancer.

Mother Pauline's nurse and companion at her bedside
was her dear younger blood sister, Sister Giuseppina
Visintainer. She had entered the convent a few years after
Mother Pauline. Sister Giuseppina would die the year
after Mother Pauline.

A young novice, Sister Theresina, also hovered about
Mother at every opportunity. She was Mother Pauline's
niece. Mother Pauline had told Theresina, "I will not die
until you are professed. I want to be there—in the chapel
on the great day of your profession." On June 29, 1941,
Sister Theresina made her profession and Mother Pauline
was there!

One year before her death, Mother Pauline had become
very ill and could not go to chapel for Holy Mass and
Communion. Early one morning, while all the sisters were
in chapel, the door of Mother Pauline's room opened and
a woman holding the hand of a beautiful child entered.
Behind the woman and child followed a man who looked
like the statue of St. Joseph in the convent chapel. The
man lifted the child in his arms and carried him closer
to the bed. The woman spoke to Mother Pauline and said,
"I know you love my Baby, Jesus. Soon you will be with
us forever in the kingdom of love. Your pain will bear
fruit in union with my Son."

On the 7th day of July, the following year, her condition worsened. The chaplain, Fr. Deltoro, gave Mother
absolution and the Papal Benediction at the hour of

death. All the Sisters were surrounding Mother's room, praying and singing hymns. The chaplain told them not to crowd the room, but to go to the chapel and pray for her.

Mother Pauline was still conscious, and in a very weak voice she said to the Sisters, "Pray to the sweet Heart of Jesus and Mary. Praise be the Divine Heart of Jesus, for He has heard my plea. Jesus, take my heart. You are my Salvation, my Redeemer, my Love. I want to do Your holy will. Make my faith strong in this hour of my death."

After the effort of speaking, she seemed to go into a kind of ecstasy and began saying, "Have mercy! Have mercy! I love you! I love you, my Jesus! Mary, my mother, take my hand and lead me home."

At 5 o'clock on the morning of July 8, 1942, Mother Pauline entered the kingdom of everlasting life. She was 76 years old. So it was that Mother Pauline was called by God. It was her last agony and her greatest ecstasy.

The simple funeral of Mother Pauline took place on July 10, 1942 in the Grand Chapel of the Holy Family in the motherhouse complex. Her request for simplicity was respected as the archbishop and the Sisters planned the liturgy for the Mother Foundress.

Archbishop Alfonesca DeSilva, Archbishop of São Paulo, was celebrant. In attendance were 72 priests and many hundreds of Sisters from the congregation and from other orders.

The day of the funeral was cold, windy and cloudy. We must remember that the month of July in Brazil is the middle of winter. Archbishop DeSilva, in his homily during the Solemn Pontifical Requiem Mass, said to the Little Sisters, "My daughters, do not cry over this death because your venerable Mother is a true saint. Her life was a long poem of marvels and humility, of simplicity and abnegation, of generosity and love. A mystical poem of pure love of God, of total abandonment to divine providence. Her life is a song of Christian charity, trust in God's unfailing grace, and a model of the blessings and beauty of religious life."

The archbishop completed the funeral rites with these words: "The greatest good you can do now for the soul of your Mother Foundress is to conserve the spirit of charity in your congregation. The Little Sisters must follow the way of their foundress, who said constantly, 'Charity, charity, charity!' "

A young novice observed that Mother Pauline was humble in death as she was in life, comparing the grand funeral of Mother Vincent and the simple rites of Mother Pauline.

Thousands of letters came from all over Brazil lauding Mother Pauline and praising her work. There were poems of gratitude and love for this servant of God from the simple and great people whom she touched with her dynamic faith and love.

After the death of Mother Pauline, many people began visiting her grave. The place of Mother's burial became a sort of popular shrine for the poor of São Paulo. They placed written requests for favors and prayers of thanksgiving upon her tomb along with a great number of flowers each day.

CHAPTER 17

The Road to Beatification

After the death of Mother Pauline, each Sister and novice had stories to tell of their experiences with the caring and loving Mother Pauline. This author had the privilege of speaking to the Sisters who had lived and worked with her. The Sisters who remembered her were then young novices in the novitiate of São Paulo at the motherhouse. Most of them are now in retirement in the beautiful home for the aged Sisters. Since it would be impossible to tell every incident, only a few will be mentioned here.

Sister Incarnata said that at the time she was a novice, Mother would visit each Sister every day, especially if she noticed that a Sister was sick or experiencing difficulty with the religious life. "I became very ill when I was a novice and Mother came twice a day to comfort and encourage me. She offered prayers and the strength of her presence. One day I said to Mother, 'I want to die now, as a novice, because I am afraid that I will not persevere as a Sister.'"

Mother Pauline said to Sister Incarnata, "You are not going to die now as a novice. You must live to work for Jesus. Do not be selfish! Jesus needs you. You must not think only of yourself. You are being made a Sister for others. After you are better, I want you to go to Vigolo for a retreat and make a novena to Our Lady of Lourdes.

I want you to stay there and pray. She will show you the reason that you must be a Little Sister of the Immaculate Conception."

"After saying these words to me, Mother embraced and kissed me, making the sign of the cross upon my forehead." The aged Sister continued, "Mother told me what to do. I went to Vigolo and even now, I have the strength and courage to know and to love and to serve my Lord. Our Lady showed me the way through Mother Pauline's advice."

Sister Assunta told this story. "When I was a novice, I was a crybaby because one day I was unable to do the work assigned to me by my superior. I tried, but after not being able to do it, I began to cry in the corner of the kitchen. Mother Pauline came past the kitchen and saw me crying in the corner. She asked me what the problem was and I told her I used to do this work with another Sister, but now I could not do it alone."

Mother said to the little novice, "Come, I will help you. I will show you that you are surely able to do it. You must have confidence in yourself. With God's help you can do all things. Nothing is impossible! You will soon be a bride of Christ!"

Sister Assunta goes on to say, "Mother stayed with me for two hours and taught me how to do the work by myself. She gave me confidence which, thank God, I have to this day."

Sister Rita tells of an event toward the end of Mother's life which illustrates her desire to serve others and diminish her own importance. Since Mother Pauline insisted on working each day, Mother General assigned Sister Rita to assist her. Mother Pauline told Sister Rita, "My dear, I appreciate your energy and work, but you certainly have many other things you can do. As for me, I can work alone until the Lord tells me to stop. I need very little to sustain me. God left me one good arm and a mouth, so I can still do something for His honor and glory."

The centenary of the birth of Mother Pauline was celebrated December 16, 1965. The congregation had grown by then to 1,153 Sisters, 328 novices, and 224 candidates in the 35 states of Brazil. The superior general, Mother Paola Maria Della Santissima, and the cardinal archbishop, Archbishop Agnello Rossi, petitioned the Holy See for permission to exhume the body of Mother Pauline.

Many miracles were being performed through the intercession of Mother Pauline. The Holy See declared her Venerable and gave permission for her body to be placed in the Chapel of the motherhouse in São Paulo.

The sacred Tribunal of the Congregation of Saints opened the cause of her beatification and canonization on May 16, 1966.

One of the outstanding miracles that led to her beatification was the healing of a young boy's leg. The boy had a withered and paralyzed leg for which the doctors could do nothing. When he was five years old, his mother dedicated him to Mother Pauline with prayer and supplication. After one year, while the lad was with his mother at the tomb of Mother Pauline, his leg began an extraordinary healing process before the eyes of about sixty laypeople and Sisters.

The doctors in Brazil verified the unexplainable growth of the leg with documentation and x-rays. Today the boy has full use of his foot and leg.

The second authenticated miracle was that of a Mrs. DeSouza, who after the birth of her baby began to hemorrhage profusely on the operating table. The doctors had given her up for dead, when two surgeons noticed that the flow of blood was stopping while the woman called out the name of Mother Pauline. In their documentation, the doctors noted that Mrs. DeSouza would surely have died due to the terrible loss of blood if there had not been a supernatural intervention.

On October 18, 1991, our Holy Father, John Paul II, beatified Mother Pauline. She is now known as Blessed Pauline of the Agonizing Heart of Jesus.

The author accompanied Mother Pauline's cousins, Albert and Louis Visintainer, with their families and American devotees, to Florianopolis, Santa Catarina in Brazil for the beatification ceremony.

The celebration was held in the magnificent oceanside park in Florianopolis. 700,000 people crowded the park and surrounding areas. The weather was cold, damp and rainy as the wind blew from the ocean, yet the enthusiasm, the warmth, and the joy of the people suffused the area with the gentle sunshine of the Brazilian people.

Rousing hymns and shouts of "Viva Madre Paulina!" throughout the ceremony brought joy to our Holy Father who said that Mother Pauline provided the "sunshine of the spirit" for the day.

Mother Pauline is the first citizen of Brazil to be beatified. From the age of ten she saw herself as a Brazilian. She will be the first citizen saint of that vast third world country familiar with hardship and sacrifice.

Mother Pauline always said, "My only joy is to do the work of my Savior. I trust only in Him. Nothing more but Jesus!"

Appendix I

Today

In 1965, on the occasion of the centenary of the birth of Mother Pauline, a granite and marble tower was erected with a bronze bust of Mother Pauline under the dome. The monument was built on the land of the Visintainer farm given to the congregation many years ago by Mother Pauline's father, Napoleone Visintainer. The farm is located between the village of Vigolo and the town of Nova Trento. In 1975, the walls of the monument, surrounding the tower, were tiled with lovely mosaics depicting the life of Mother Pauline.

Two miles from the tower monument is the "Hill of Mother Pauline." At the very summit of the small mountain, overlooking the rich, green fields in which she worked, is a huge bronze statue of Mother Pauline with a garden hoe in one hand and a cross in the other. During Mother Pauline's time, a large cross had been erected upon the mountain by the people of Vigolo. Often, Mother Pauline could be found at the foot of that cross, weeping and praying for others, seeking conversions of the lost.

One enters the road to the mountain through a grand arch of concrete. The inscription on the arch reads, "Pray that you will follow Christ to the glory He has prepared for you." The road that leads to the top of the hill winds around the mountain, and at each kilometer of the climb, there is a tile mosaic depicting a significant moment in the life of Mother Pauline and the history of the congregation.

At the top of the hill are three fountains of pure spring water which the pilgrims take and have blessed at the weekly Mass in the Church of St. George and the sanctuary of Our Lady of Lourdes at the bottom of the hill.

To this day the Sisters of Mother Pauline's congregation celebrate the Feast of Our Lady of Lourdes with special solemnity. I, the author, was at the motherhouse of the Little Sisters of the Immaculate Conception during the Feast of Our Lady of Lourdes in 1993. There was a huge gathering of Sisters from all the provinces of Brazil. A solemn Mass and Feast was celebrated in honor of Our Lady.

A novena of Our Lady of Lourdes is prayed in each convent of the community using the special community prayer book. This Marian devotion is an inheritance from Mother Pauline's intense devotion to the Blessed Mother from the first days at Vigolo.

Next to the Church of St. George in Vigolo is a replica of the first one-room convent and hospital of Amabile and Virginia.

In the city of Nova Trento, about one mile from Vigolo, is the second foundation, which is a combination chapel, convent, and hospital. This building has been made into a museum by the Little Sisters in honor of Mother Pauline. The silk mill in Nova Trento is no longer in operation. However, the congregation has restored the mill as a museum with the original tools and implements used by Mother Pauline.

As I walked around the museum, I was amazed at the immense amount of work that must have been done with these almost primitive tools. The plaques on the walls were commendations in many languages. I was tremendously surprised to see one in English, a Certificate of Honor from the Exposition of St. Louis, Missouri, in the United States.

Today there is a large compound on the grounds of the motherhouse in São Paulo. The land that once was used for fields to raise food for the Sisters and orphans now includes an orphanage for boys and girls, a secondary school, and the College and University of San Carlos. The grounds of the motherhouse are still extensive, even though the Sisters sold much of the land for commercial use. The old silk mill buildings still exist, but they are rented to a trucking company, which uses them for storage. This area used to be in the suburbs, but is now part of the urban crowding of São Paulo.

The chapel at the motherhouse is now used for large gatherings of the community and for weekly Masses in honor of Mother Pauline. There have been many renovations to the chapel and many buildings have been constructed in the complex surrounding it. The gigantic wooden statue of St. Joseph that had been the centerpiece of the old church remains in the chapel today, one hundred years later. The capacity of the chapel is 800 people and is the place where Mother Pauline's body rests.

The author of this book was in Braganza at St. Vincent de Paul Asylum, and I was appalled at the poverty and suffering I witnessed. I was depressed for days after spending a few hours there. The Sisters who work there are true Christian heroes. Despite 90 °F temperatures, they use wood-burning stoves for cooking in the kitchen. Those Sisters are enveloped in heat which I likened to a sauna. This author was inspired and amazed by the wonderful work of the Sisters in that house of mercy and love. One can only imagine how it was in 1909 during Mother Pauline's time.

There is today a magnificent mural of Mother Pauline working among the poor and suffering in Braganza. The artist worked in beautiful tiles and placed them on a surviving wall of the old hospital depicting Mother Pauline's love and care. The mural was given by the grateful community of the people of Braganza.

Today Mother Pauline's congregation numbers 1,892 Sisters, 130 novices, and 300 aspirants. Foundations are in every state of Brazil, and in Argentina, Chile, Nicaragua, and Italy. They are in Chad, Zambia, and Mozambique in Africa.

Mother Pauline chose her cousin, Albert Visintainer of Mount Carmel, Pennsylvania, to be her messenger in the United States. Through a long series of improbable events, Albert came to know of his blood relative and the congregation which she founded. It was through Albert that we came to know this humble saint.

At the beatification in Brazil, Albert was given a first class relic of Mother Pauline. Only three first class relics were made available: Albert received one, our Holy Father received one for the Vatican, and the institute which Mother Pauline founded shared a relic for each province.

The body of Mother Pauline of the Agonizing Heart of Jesus is being carefully and scientifically renovated and preserved in Verona, Italy. The body will be taken back to São Paulo, Brazil, encased in a glass and gold sarcophagus.

The glass coffin will be hermetically sealed but her body will be visible for the veneration of the faithful. The coffin will be returned to its place before the altar in the Grand Chapel of the Holy Family at the motherhouse in Ipiranga, São Paulo.

The enormous cost of this project was funded by Albert Visintainer and the American devotees of Mother Pauline. A plaque with the names of the group who assisted in this work will be placed in the chapel.

The Sisters could not afford to spend such a large sum on this project, and besides, they felt Mother Pauline would not want such a grand resting place. However, after much urging, the Sisters agreed. The Council of the Institute after accepting this gift said, in the words of Mother Pauline, "We cannot repay you, so we will let God do it."

APPENDIX II

Historical and Family Background

Vigolo Vattaro, Blessed Pauline's birthplace, was a town of approximately two thousand people in the South Tyrol. Geographically and linguistically, it was a part of Italy. However, in 1875, it was politically under the old Austrian and Hungarian Empire. The capital of the province was Trent, an ancient Roman town with a rich and glorious history.

The history of the South Tyrol is one of wars, destruction, revenge and the greediness of foreign domination. Christianity reached this area about the year 300 A.D. with the arrival of the great apostle and martyr, St. Vigilius, the first bishop of the upper region of the Adige River. After the fall of the Roman Empire, the Tridentine area was occupied by the invading barbarians until the year 952, when Otto I, King of Germany, attached the area to the Kingdom of Germany. The Holy Roman Empire held the area of Trent with the rule of the prince-bishops until the Counts of Tyrol assumed rule in 1240. (Tyrol was an ancient castle near Merano.)

In 1363, the Countess of Maultasch, who was the heiress of the Tyrol, married the Hapsburg Duke, Rudolph IV of Austria, and Trent passed to the Austrian domination of the Alto Adige area. The Germanization of the North and South Tyrol began at this time. For over one hundred years, the prince-bishops of Trent were Germans, and many German families settled in the South Tyrol. It was at this time that the Visintainer family ancestors came to the area of Trent. The first documents that speak of the Visintainer family date from 1491. Prince-Bishop Frederick Vanga began the mining of silver and he called many experienced miners from Germany. When the inhabitants of the South Tyrol, who were of German descent, were given the choice of adopting the Italian language, those of the area near present day Merano, Bressanone and Bolzano kept the German language, while those farther south opted for Italian.

The Visintainer family ventured farther south and purchased land to begin an agricultural way of life. The Micheloni family, also ancestors of Blessed Pauline, had always been in Vigolo according to the parish archives from the most ancient times.

Paternal Grandparents of Blessed Pauline

Alessandro Visintainer, son of Francesco Visintainer and Catarina Angeli, was born in Ischia (Pergine, Valsugana) in 1803. He moved to Vigolo Vattaro in 1820 where he lived until his death in 1860.

Lucia Margarita Micheloni, daughter of Antonio and Girolama Zamboni, was born in Vigolo Vattaro in 1805. She lived in Vigolo Vattaro until her death in 1877.

Alessandro and Lucia were married on the 4th of February, 1828. Ten children, who became known as the "Lissandris;' were born from this marriage. Among the ten children was Antonio Napoleone, the father of Blessed Pauline. He was born on January 7, 1840 in Vigolo Vattaro. Also among these ten children was Antonio Guiseppe, the grandfather of Albert Visintainer of Mount Carmel, Pennsylvania.

Maternal Grandparents of Blessed Pauline

Giovanni Battista Pianezzer, son of Antonio Pianezzer and and Anna Dallabrida, was born July 23, 1815 in

Vigolo Vattaro.

Domenica Lucia Zamboni, daughter of Antonio Zamboni and Domenica Andreata, was born January 23, 1817 in Vigolo Vattaro.

Gionvanni Pianezzer and Domenica Zamboni were married on January 26, 1839 in Vigolo Vattaro. From this union were born eight children. The oldest was Anna, born on October 16, 1840 in Vigolo Vattaro. She was the mother of Blessed Pauline.

Antonio Napoleone Visintainer married Anna Pianezzer on Feburary 6, 1864 in Vigolo Vattaro. The witnesses for this marriage were Andrea Bailoni and Giovanni Bridi. The priest who performed the marriage was the assistant pastor of the parish of St. George, Fr. Vigilio Luchi. Napoleone was 24 years old and Anna was 23. Fourteen children were born from this marriage, of whom eight survived. Amabile Lucia Visintainer was the second child and first daughter, born December 16, 1865 in Vigolo Vattaro.

Vigolo and Nova Trento

Brazil was discovered by the Portuguese in 1500 and it remained a colony of Portugal until the Napoleonic Wars when the royal family of Portugal was forced to immigrate to Brazil.

In 1820, King John VI returned to Portugal, leaving his son, King Pedro, as his heir. In 1822, King Pedro proclaimed independence from Portugal and he was declared King Pedro I. When his father became ill, he returned to Portugal and his son was crowned King Pedro II. He ruled until 1889, when Brazil was declared a republic. In the same year, 1889, all slaves in Brazil were emancipated.

In 1874, King Pedro II had signed a contract with Commander Joaquim Caetano Pinto stating that within ten years, 100,000 Europeans would immigrate to Brazil. This contract was in turn signed by the groups of people who came from the Tyrol, among whom were the people from Vigolo Vattaro.

From July 6 to September 25, 1875, 402 people left Vigolo Vattaro, Italy. The following families went to Brazil: Nicoletti, Pianezzer, Giacomelli, Zamboni, Bianchini, Sadler, Bailoni, Curzel, Sgnaldo, Moratelli, Perotti, Bartolomeotti, Visintainer, Dallabrida, Furlani, Bridi, Tamanini, Franzoi and Fracalossi.

When these families first arrived in Brazil, the places they settled, Nova Trento and Vigolo, were in the Archdiocese of Rio de Janeiro. Geographically it was a massive diocese, covering many states in Brazil. Because of the huge size of the diocese, pastors of the churches and missions were delegated by the bishop to confirm the faithful.

By 1895, this huge archdiocese was divided. Nova Trento was now in the Diocese of Curitiba, which encompassed the states of Paraná and Santa Catarina.

By 1909, the Diocese of Curitiba was further subdivided, and Nova Trento was now in the Diocese of Florianoplis.

Some Key People

Blessed Pauline's best friend, Virginia Nicolodi, was born in Aldeno, Italy on August 3, 1864, and lived in Vigolo with her parents, Francesco and Angela (Dallago). She was about a year older than Mother Pauline.

Sabina Bottamedi was the daughter of John Bottamedi and Julia Cornali. She was born in the lower valley of Nova Trento, Brazil, on December 18, 1879.

The second novitiate, called the Novitiate of the Holy Purification, began on February 2, 1896. The girls in that class were: Theresa Valiati, Virginia Cestari, Madalena Tamanini, Anna Kuntze, Maria Venoti, Anna Dalsasso, Maria Pezzi, Lucia Rodi, Antonietta Moratelli, Maria Fracalossi and Antonietta Mazzarolla.

Dates of Key Events in the Life of Mother Pauline

December 16, 1865	Born in Vigolo Vattaro, Trento.
December 17, 1865	Baptized by Fr. Antonio Ferrari. Godparents: Carlo Dallabrida and Orsola Tonezzer.
April 27, 1873	Confirmed. Louise Bailoni, godmother.
August 1, 1875	First wave of emigration.
September 25, 1875	Visintainers leave for Brazil via Le Havre.
late October, 1875	Leave Le Havre for Brazil.
mid November, 1875	Arrival in Itajai.
December 24, 1876	The men return to Itajai after 6 months away.
August 7, 1886	Death of Anna, Amabile's mother.
April 19, 1888	Fr. Servanzi transferred.
June 26, 1890	Little Chapel blessed.
July 22, 1890	Move into cabin on Napoleone's farm.
September 8, 1891	Theresa Maoli joins the two.
February 12, 1894	The move to Nova Trento.
February 4, 1895	Fr. Rocchi announces his transfer.
March 2, 1895	Fr. Rocchi leaves—Fr. Rossi takes over.
August 25, 1895	Bishop gives approbation to new community.
December 7, 1895	Investiture of the girls.
February 2, 1896	New novitiate class begins.
October 29, 1896	Silk mill begun.
January 7, 1897	New orphanage dedicated.
December 15, 1897	Catherine Tonet comes to Sister Pauline.
1899	Becomes an authentic religious congregation.
March 19, 1900	Sabina exorcised.
July 7, 1900	Leo XIII sends blessing.
1900	Four Polish girls join.
February 2, 1903	Fr. Rossi moves from Nova Trento.
June 1903	Fr. Rossi asks Sisters to come to São Paulo.

Love's Harvest

July 17, 1903	Sister Pauline and companions leave Nova Trento.
July 19, 1903	They arrive at the port of Itajai and sail for Santos.
November 22, 1903	Vicar General celebrates Mass in Ipiranga.
December 7, 1903	Sisters move into house in Ipiranga.
1905	Bishop Barros' ship sinks.
August 12-19, 1905	Bishop Duarte visits Nova Trento.
August 13, 1909	Mother Pauline visits Bishop Duarte.
1909	Mother Pauline removed as Mother General.
August 29, 1909	Fr. Rossi named co-founder, Mother Pauline Mother Foundress.
September 3, 1909	Mother Pauline leaves São Paulo for Braganza.
July 12, 1910	20th anniversary of founding.
March 6, 1911	Napoleone, Mother Pauline's father, dies.
July 22, 1917	Mother Matilda (Virginia Nicolodi) dies.
1919	2nd Chapter calls Mother Pauline back to motherhouse.
August 13, 1921	Fr. Rossi ill and brought to motherhouse.
October 30, 1921	Fr. Rossi dies.
September 28, 1931	Mother Vincent (Sabina Bottamedi) dies.
March 27, 1932	Receive Decree of Praise for Mother Vincent from Rome.
1938	Mother Pauline's eyes affected by diabetes.
1940	Little Sister's celebrate 50th anniversary with Mother Pauline.
March 2, 1941	Mother Pauline confined to bed.
March 17, 1941	She receives Last Rites.
May, June 1941	Doctors discover Mother Pauline has pulmonary cancer.
June 29, 1941	Mother Pauline is present for Sister Theresina's profession.
July 7, 1942	Her condition worsens.
July 8, 1942	Mother Pauline dies.
July 10, 1942	Simple funeral at the motherhouse.
December 16, 1965	Centenary of Mother Pauline's birth celebrated.
May 16, 1966	Her cause for beatification is opened.
October 18, 1991	Mother Pauline beatified by Pope John Paul II in Florianopolis.
December 7, 1995	The 100th anniversary investiture and personal dedication of the three girls as Sisters.